MEDIAPOLIS

MEDIAPOLIS

Popular Culture and the City

Alex de Jong
Marc Schuilenburg

010 Publishers, Rotterdam 2006

This book has been made possible by the financial support of
the Netherlands Foundation for Visual Arts, Design and Architecture,
and the Netherlands Architecture Fund

Reading committee: Prof. F.L.H. Alkemade, Dr. R.A. de Brabander and Dr. J.F.F. Raessens
Text editing: Hanneke de Man
Translation from the Dutch: George Hall
Design: Simon Davies, Rotterdam
3D cover illustration: Jeroen Beltman
Print: Die Keure, Brugge

ISBN 978-90-6450-628-4

A Dutch edition of this book was published under the title
Mediapolis. Populaire cultuur en de stad (ISBN 978-90-6450-633-8)

Contents

[V

Contents

Contents

PART THREE

Nodal Urbanity 109

CHAPTER 1

FROM GENIUS TO SCENIUS 111

Contents

CHAPTER 2

THE CITY IN A FLOODED WORLD 130

POSTSCRIPT 151

Introduction

The bottom of our money bag is in sight and problems are piling up.
Sure, our financial experts did warn us. Lending large sums of money against exaggerated interest rates – that had to go wrong. But the city leaves us no other option. Our debts can only be paid if the city continues to grow. And new residents can only be attracted if there are facilities such as electricity, water, motorways, and adequate public transport. Moreover, the citizens are not particularly keen about an increase in municipal taxes. What are those financial fusspots complaining about? After all, in the current global economy, everything depends on population growth and the advent of new companies. Are they fully aware that those who do not invest will fall behind in the march of civilization? Only daring growth scenarios, inventiveness, the necessary nerve, skilled personnel, and lots of luck can lay down a breeding ground from which the city can evolve. Impressive bridges and parks, eye-catching skyscrapers and striking museums – that is what we want. It would be better if our advisors would formulate plans to generate the necessary income. It actually began to go wrong with the construction of the new seaport. And it was completely out of order when we discovered that it is almost impossible to construct roads and railway lines through the hilly landscape to the harbour. We now have a marvellous harbour but no hinterland. There is a baseball stadium able to accommodate 80,000 fans. Unfortunately, the stadium lies in a run-down neighbourhood where crime is the favourite sport of the people. But be fair! Fire stations, police

stations and hospitals are nothing compared to skyscrapers and modern topsport arenas. The degeneration of the public space and the use of municipal funds for capital-devouring mega-projects have turned the city into a ghost town. People are leaving in droves, heading for other cities. Bankruptcy of the city seems inevitable. We shall soon lose our job as Mayor.

Fortunately, the scenario described above remains limited to the pixels on our computer screens. The drama is a part of the game *SimCity 4* created by Electronic Arts (2003). The starting points of modern urban design have become algorithms in a game that evokes a true Faustian feeling among the players. Although the competence to change the city radically is far more extensive that that of 'real' mayors in New York and Berlin, the activities in the virtual environment of *Sim-City* are unmistakably related to events in physical space. *Sim-City* allows us to enter the minds of the urban designers and architects such as Baron Haussmann and Le Corbusier. We experience what the city architect Robert Moses must have felt when he constructed his parkways in New York in the 1930s and various neighbourhoods had to be obliterated to create the new metropolis. His motto was: '*When you operate in an overbuilt metropolis you have to hack your way through with a meat axe.*' [1]

10]

We are surrounded by the sounds and images of pop culture. The popular media have the world in a tight grip, the virtual representation of the city is one form of expression of this. In this context, the Indian anthropologist Arjun Appadurai speaks of 'mediascapes'. Mediascapes refer to the extremely diverse media (newspapers, television, internet, films, etc.) that produce, disseminate and process information, and to the force of the images they create. [2] If we only look at games on internet, the influence of popular culture becomes crystal-clear. Around six million people pay contribution to gain access to the parallel worlds of online games such as *Lineage II* (NCsoft, 2004) and *World of Warcraft* (Electronic Arts, 1994). [3] In these synthetic environments, imagination is a collective and social happening. Elves, dragons and sinister alter egos fight for a place in the realm of Azeroth. Magic swords, shields and special powers are stolen here. People kill players and group together to earn money in order to buy items such as weapons and clothing, which are necessary to survive. Once imagination has taken over, it not only offers an escape from the daily grind but also functions as a powerful fuel for new forms of communal action. Absorbed by their virtual characters, players marry online and offline. 'Real' people earn a month's income with the sale of virtual objects, and players turn out to be the architects of the digital environment in which they hang around for hours every day. Is it necessary to state that popular culture is more than trivial or banal entertainment? Just as in 'normal' life, the mediascapes also have their exceptional forms of social traffic and collective codes of conduct, powerful economies flourish, and there is a mixture of regulation and mutual conflict management.

A POP PHILOSOPHY OF THE POLIS

Expressions of popular culture fit into the electronic globalization that the German philosopher Peter Sloterdijk regards as the third stage of the globalization process. In his study *Sphären* (Spheres) Sloterdijk speaks of a multiple globalization. Beginning in Greek Antiquity with the charting of the cosmos, it took on a territorial guise with the voyage of Columbus to America in 1492, and it now assumes the form of a digital globalization. To many, this last process contains a magical promise. However, the sociologist Vincent Mosco warns that expectations of new media, such as internet, consistently lead to the same myths.[4] Every introduction of a medium evokes a phase of euphoria, a hymn to the unprecedented possibilities that this technology has in store for the world. No medium whatsoever can bring this promise to fruition. Nevertheless, an analysis of the influence of popular culture cannot afford to ignore the role of technology.

[11

For several years, game-technology has been an integral component of various practices. For example, it is used by a new generation of spatial planners and urban designers for the co-ordination and planning of large-scale urban areas.[5] But the socialization of the technology of pop culture has not remained limited to our urban planning. Well-known games are deployed by military forces in various countries to train soldiers for 'real' warfare.

The representation of popular culture exercises an indelible and not-to-be-underestimated influence on everyday life. This observation is a good reason to examine our physical environment from a different viewpoint. We take as our starting point the virtual and sonic environments of popular media such as games and electronic music. How does this popular culture influence everyday reality? An increasing number of games, including well-known games such as *America's Army* (U.S. Army, 2002) and *Grand Theft Auto* (Rockstar Games, 2005), are largely set in an urban environment. In that context, the players learn to survive collectively, build up a career in the underworld, or live in a neighbourhood 'where there is always plenty going on and everything depends on your reputation'. Taking pop culture seriously raises the issue of whether or not we also learn to handle the dangers present in the public space of the physical city better by playing First Person Shooter games. In addition, there are the sounds and rhythms of pop music, which stimulate people worldwide to converge around all kinds of musical genres with their own codes, clothes, and gestures.

We use the term 'pop philosophy' to refer to the approach that uses popular media as material to analyse the contours of our everyday environment. This philosophy opens a playful space in the margins of the primarily academically tinted discourse of the city. In *Mediapolis*, this takes place by investigating the representation of urban space in pop culture. What does urban reality look like in those virtual and sonic environments and how does this affect our physical reality?

The representation of urban space in popular media produces many examples worth noting. Almost everyone will be familiar with Steven Spielberg's staging of the cyber city in the film *Minority Report* (2002). Three years prior to beginning the production of this film, Spielberg invited sixteen specialists, including William Mitchell who was the author of *City of Bits*, and Peter Calthorpe, an urban theorist, to think about the future of the city. The film unmistakably shows that popular culture in the past few decades has offered increasingly complex images, information and interpretations of all kinds of social developments. Accordingly, the film forms the proof that a popular medium can also function as an information carrier of our culture. But which urban life actually goes on in the realm of pop culture? Which rules and regulations apply there and which punishments are imposed if the rules are violated?

In order to answer these questions, we appeal in this book to the various meanings of the world *polis*. Besides the territorial determination of the city and its surroundings, the concept also refers to a religious and political unit (*omonoia* [Gr.], *concordia* [Lat]). In this way, the *polis* embodies the living space of a group of people who are linked by means of their origins, beliefs, and political convictions. But what is the meaning of *polis* in a world that is occupied by the images and information of popular culture, a world in which the city plays an increasingly important role?

DROPPING SCIENCE

Hardly a day goes by that we don't watch a film, play a game, or listen to pop music. The presence of these media not only forms a gauge for the significance and value of current events, they also display continual movement between various dimensions, such as from the virtual to the real and from the real to the virtual. This book aligns itself with this phenomenon by using popular culture as a springboard for thinking about the changes that are taking place in our daily lives. The first part of this book, *Virtual Urbanity*, demonstrates that the struggle for public space takes place in an arena that is embedded in virtuality. This situation offers creative opportunities but can also have repressive consequences. If we look at the current culture of security, we observe the increasing militarization of public space. A military control net has been thrown across the city and the mesh is being drawn tighter and tighter, leading to an altered experience of one's own identity as well as the installation of a specific regime of rules and sanctions. Renowned war games such as *America's Army* and *Full Spectrum Warrior* (THQ, 2004) which are played worldwide, represent these radical changes better than the latest police report or academic manuscripts. These games indicate how the militarization of life has become the most important input of a culture that is oriented toward security. These same war games describe how architecture and public space manifest themselves in a society that has been engaged in transforming itself from a structure in which everything depended on discipline to one in which 'control' is currently the key word. In a control culture, the separate spaces once inhabited by the institutions of the disciplinary society have been bundled together to accommodate current social functions such as shopping, living, work, and education. The roots of this architecture lie both in the *company town* of the industrial era and in the *compound* of internationally operating enterprises. This architecture manifests itself in its most mod-

[13

ern form in Asian cities like Hong Kong, Shanghai and Beijing, where *Urban Containers* rise at infrastructural nodes.

The first part of *Mediapolis* ends with new forms of resistance as seen in Arabic war games. The notion of resistance is always connected to activities on the streets. But Arabic games turn out not only to contain hostility-based identities, they also give the players a communal identity so that they can rebel in a virtual space against the dominance of Israel and the United States.

In the second part, *Sonic Urbanity*, we observe that one must distinguish various spaces in order to genuinely understand the process of urbanization. For this reason we introduce 'sonic thinking' in relation to the city. Since we seem to be convinced that right-minded people first look and then listen, sound is more often experienced as being a source of nuisance. The concepts of Peter Sloterdijk offer a starting point for a positive approach to sound. Sound creates large interior spatialities that are not immediately and permanently determined. The 'Techno' electronic dance music from Detroit and the 'Urban' mediagenic youth culture demonstrate that our physical environment can evaporate in an audiovisual sphere of meanings. In this ephemeral situation, the city can be actualized in an unannounced and unexpected way. In creating a sonic spatiality, popular music proves that sound also has political significance, in other words, it is engaged with the design of life. A sonic spatiality contains both the spatial and the social processes that accompany sound. People are mutually connected in a sonic spatiality worldwide, and enter into social relationships and contacts. This is why the technique of sampling is brought into association with a line of flight or an 'away from here' attitude for spread-out communities who converge around the sounds and beat rates of various music styles.

In the third part, *Nodal Urbanity*, we return to the virtual world to describe a radical-democratic form of productive co-operation generated in that environment. What happens when we take the production of many as a starting point, rather than that of the ingenious soloist? With the introduction of the concept of 'scenius', this last part describes the possibilities of giving shape to a virtual environment with the help of an interactive strategy of 'many-to-many'. One of the most important features of the scenius is the interaction between the initiators, the fans and the users who gather around a shared interest or specific goal. The interaction between these three parties is

14]

the driving force behind this unique model. Can the scenius also be deployed in the design of the physical environment of the city, with buildings, streets and squares?

To unravel the complexity of urban space and to obtain a better understanding of the diversity of ideas in pop culture, we conclude *Mediapolis* with a description of four mutually interacting processes that crisscross urban space: virtuality, interactivity, connectivity, and multimediality. We refer to the form in which the convergence of these processes is given shape as 'nodal urbanity'. It is the name for a pulsating urban life which cannot be further defined in purely physical terms. In other words, the geographical space of the city must be regarded as an open field or as a medial infrastructure that can constantly actualize itself.

BUT WHERE DO THOSE CITIES COME FROM? [15

Studying popular media offers a perfect excuse for roaming around in new worlds, images, music, and 'grand narratives'. Is there anything more pleasant than spending a weekend in *Liberty City* in *Grand Theft Auto* or dancing to the latest sounds from London? Nonetheless, this book does not wish to be seen as an attempt to make well-known theories about our environment accessible to a wide public by illustrating them with attractive examples from popular culture. The basic idea of *Mediapolis* is that the popular media environments, in which technical, cultural and economic changes join in a unique way, offer an opportunity to approach our living environment from a different angle. The information, ideas and opinions of pop culture are connected to actuality by means of the question concerning our cultural and political situation. We wish to understand what is happening in virtual and sonic environments and, if other concepts come to the fore or if deviating futures are displayed, we can at least try to use those ideas and vistas as tools for thinking about the dynamics and potential of our direct environment. That is why the words of the Italian futurist Antonio Sant'Elia in his *Manifesto of Futurist Architecture* (1914) remain topical: '*Every generation must build its own city.*'

VIRTUAL URBANITY

PART ONE

CHAPTER 1

The Militarization of Life

ON Independence Day (4 July) 2002, eight months before the United States invaded Iraq, the American army issued a computer game entitled *America's Army: Operations*. The game, which cost the army more than 6.3 million dollars, is a 'first-person shooter'. By means of an internet site especially set up for this purpose, players worldwide are informed that they can replay the armed battles of the American army. An exceptional feature of the game is the fact that it need not be purchased in a shop. Everyone can play *America's Army*. For free! The game can be downloaded from the website of the same name. In the first two weeks after its launch more than one million people logged in on one of the servers. More than four million players have now registered. The game is played by several hundred thousand people every day. As a consequence of this overwhelming success, the American army has established its own development studio in which dozens of people are engaged in improving *America's Army*. It is not without reason that the army of the United States has adopted the multiplayer and joystick technologies of games and game computers. The fight of heavily armed troops against foreign militias, drugs criminals or armed terrorists is a favourite theme of many game players. However, never before has a national army been responsible for the development and distribution of a game with the aims of recruiting soldiers and of giving citizens insight and a virtual role in the 'best army in the world'.

With countless young people waging war on the internet daily, the issue of the role of these games in our relationship to 'the merely illusory' reality of virtuality is becoming increasingly relevant. By playing these games, are we training ourselves for an existence in an environment in which it is becoming more and more difficult to distinguish between virtual and objective reality? In order to discover how our daily lives are being influenced by this virtual reality, we must analyse the link between these two dimensions and investigate the extent of any opposition between virtual and objective reality. For this reason, we orient the first part of *Mediapolis* to the mediascapes of war games. With games as our basis, we chart three lines along which virtual reality influences our physical environment.

We cover the issue of how the activities of the game are related to the physical body of the player. Does the player become a soldier who allows his behaviour to be entirely determined by these activities? In other words, does the game make the player a military subject who shapes his actions on the basis of a specific knowledge?

In addition, we examine whether or not virtual space is a lawless or amoral universe. Is it true that players need not worry about rules and regulations and are allowed to open fire on one another at any hint of danger, without any form of self-discipline? Can life in the virtual world of video games function without rules and sanctions?

Finally, we concentrate on the architectonic setting of war games. Instead of hilly landscapes, tropical forests or the expanses of outer space, the city is increasingly the décor for the armed conflict. In popular games, densely populated streets, cluttered squares, and high-rise apartment blocks in cities such as New York and Los Angeles form the environment in which the gun battles take place. For the first time, the city is more dangerous than the surroundings. On this basis, we examine the influence of virtual space on the last issue, that concerning architecture in our physical environment.

EMPOWER YOURSELF, DEFEND FREEDOM [1]

In order to demonstrate how the virtual activities influence the personalities of the players, it is necessary to review the thriving co-operation between the games and the military industry. The tight relationship between the military structure and the entertainment industry is referred to as the 'military-entertainment complex'.[2] This complex has been shaped along various lines and is the result of developments that have their origins at the beginning of the nineteenth century. In the meantime, the military-entertainment complex has grown to become one of the important themes in our culture. As such, each war, whether this concerns the fight against drugs or the war on terrorism, has been the basis of a video game. Games are also used by the army in simulation training for soldiers. In addition, images of existing wars are fused with special effects from video games to form a new whole.

How should we regard the development that turns warfare into a game? The experiences of soldiers are exceptionally popular in the world of video games. The latest military weapons, the dangers that occur during a special mission, or the romantic feeling of 'the lads together' have great powers of attraction for young players. *Tomahawk Missile* (Electro Sport, 1980), *Missile Command* (Atari, 1980), *Armor Attack* (Vectrex, 1982), *Top Gunner* (Konami, 1986), and *Top Gun* (Konami, 1987) are early examples of games in which warfare, in the classic sense of armed struggle between two or more world powers, is simulated. The list of similar games is much longer. *Conflict: Desert Storm* (Gotham Games, 2002) is set in the first Gulf War. A player leads a commando team of four soldiers who have to carry out the missions of the operation of the same name in 1991. To ensure that the occupation of Kuwait is successfully resolved, each soldier in the elite team has unique skills. The more use he makes of these, the more effectively the unit operates within the game. *Conflict: Desert Storm II – Back To Baghdad* (Take-Two Interactive, 2003) was brought out shortly after the beginning of the second Gulf War. The *Conflict* series has now been extended with *Desert Sabre* (SCi, 2003), which replays the missions of the Desert Shield campaign, and *Missing Presumed Dead* (SCi, 2004), in which a number of soldiers are trapped behind enemy lines during the American offensive in Vietnam in 1968.

[21

The fact that warfare is a consistent source of inspiration for the issue of new games is displayed above all by the game entitled *Kuma: War* (2004), developed by *Kuma Reality* and based on topical events. The title of the games stands for *'Real War News. Real War Games'*. The company that makes the games aims at allowing the players to replay 'last week's news'. This means that the most recent war scenes from everywhere can be downloaded in the form of an action game. In this way, players from all over the world have the opportunity to participate in the American hunt for members of Al Qaeda in the Shah-i-Kot Valley in Eastern Afghanistan. But they can also feel the tension of an American soldier who is on the brink of entering the hiding place of Saddam Hussein, the former Iraqi president, to overpower him. Besides recent events such as the death of Abu Musab al-Zarqawi, the leader of the Al Qaeda terror network in Iraq, and the bloody happenings in the centre of Fallujah, *Kuma: War* does not eschew going back further in time. For example, the military actions that brought the American presidential candidate in the elections of 2002, John Kerry, a Silver Star medal have been translated into a game that can be played on the *Kuma: War* server. One can view with one's own eyes just how heroic Kerry actually was in the war in Vietnam.

Whereas *Kuma: War* uses only existing war actions as its basis for games, other games go a step further. In these games, war is no longer approached from a traditional point of view – the exercise of state violence against another state by means of military force – but the action has a more topical substantiation. The new wars against organized crime and terrorism form the background for games such as *Narc* (Midway Games, 2005), which focuses on the struggle of the American government against the drug trade. In the various versions of the game, a player can choose the role of the narcotics agents Jack Forzenski and Marcus Hill, who are engaged in a bloody conflict with the empire of a powerful drugs cartel. In the game *Max Payne* (Rockstar Games, 2003) the player fights against organized crime by teaming up with the mafia as an undercover agent. The war against the mafia is continued in *True Crime: Streets of L.A.* (Activision, 2004). Here, the player has to enter the identity of Nick Kang and defend the streets of Los Angeles against the terror of Chinese crime syndicates and the Russian mafia. And now that *Counterstrike: Source* (Valve, 2004) focuses on the war against terror in all its facets, we can unequivocally state that the games industry has reached the point at which each war has been translated into a video game.

WELCOME TO THE BATTLEZONE

The relationship between the army and the games industry does not remain limited to video games in which the player can participate in the struggle against other states, drug criminals operating worldwide, dictators, or widely disseminated terrorist networks. It is exactly because video games are so successful in presenting reality in a transparent way that they are used as training material for soldiers and officers. In these simulations of operational actions, soldiers obtain the feeling that they are actually in the real world. The Slovenian philosopher Slavoj Žižek refers to this as 'post-modern' transparency. The workings of the machine remain hidden behind the interface image in order to enable the presentation of the soldiers' experience as faithfully as possible. As a result, the digital machinery 'behind the screen' becomes completely impenetrable and invisible.[3] Because the boundaries between 'true' reality, simulation and training are becoming increasingly blurred, the medium of the games computer vanishes into thin air, as it were.

At this point we have arrived at the second aspect of co-operation between the games industry and the military industry. Games are being increasingly deployed to train soldiers in the army. Research has allegedly indicated that people who are good at playing computer games also remain more concentrated in other situations. Are gamers better soldiers? According to Chris Chambers, the assistant project manager of the *America's Army's* project, players experience the virtual reality of a game in a very intense manner: *'There's a very high level of visual acuity in game players that's different than non-players. They're good at focusing on specific things in a chaotic environment, which is an important skill in a lot of Army situations.'*[4]

Much of the technology used in video games has its origins in military research. For example, the technology of the Game Boy was funded by the Pentagon. And to ensure that the technology of Silicon Graphic's SGI, the 3-D graphics workstations on which video games are designed, was financially feasible, a great number of these were purchased by military companies such as Boeing and Lockheed-Martin.[5]

The method applied by the army to use a game as a 'real-life' simulation of war in order to be able to study it and practise in detail goes back at least two hundred years to Baron von Reisswitz's analogous *Kriegsspiel* (1811). In this scale model, the battlefield is accurately copied, and the scale of the landscape with hills, rivers, and forests is so precise that, by examining the distance and knowing the speed of their divisions, the generals could calculate the time at which the troops would come within range of enemy fire. However, for the moment at which games genuinely began to play a prominent role in the training of military personnel, we have to go to the 1980s. *Battlezone* (Atari, 1980) was the first commercial game that was used by the American army to train its soldiers. In the game designed by Ed Rotberg, the player is placed in a 3-D environment with an erupting volcano as the most striking detail. When the player is riding in his tank, the changes in the landscape give the impression that the battlefield is consistently altering. According to Rotberg, a changing environment is an absolute precondition to involve the player in the game: *'Given the technology that we had, the real challenge was how to make the game appear as if we had more technology than we did. And the question was always: How do we involve the player? Meeting those needs was where the artistry was involved in designing a game in those days.'* [6] In the rocky landscape of *Battlezone*, the vehicle can shelter behind small objects to avoid the missiles from other tanks. The player who steers the tank by means of two joysticks has only one weapon available: a large cannon by means of which he or she can destroy an enemy tank with one shot. The leadership of the American army was so impressed by the possibilities of this game that they asked the producer Atari to create a second version of the game. This fight simulator was aimed at enhancing the eye-hand co-ordination of the tank driver. In the adapted version entitled *Army Battlezone*, American soldiers can practise riding and firing in a virtual play environment.

24]

Since the success of *Army Battlezone* an increasing number of games have been converted to simulation and training material for the American army. Commercial games, too, such as *Delta Force* (NovaLogic, 1998), *Medal of Honor* (Electronic Arts, 1999), *Counterstrike* and *Operation Flashpoint* (Codemasters, 2001) have been converted to training simulations for the various sections of the American army. For example, the game *Doom* (1993), issued by id Software in the nineties, was modified by the *Marine Corps Combat and Development Command* into the training module *Marine Doom*. In *Marine Doom*, elite soldiers learn to work in teams of four. According to a spokesperson of the *Marine Corps Modeling and Simulation Management Office*, the game is extremely suited to the training of a new generation of soldiers: *'Kids who join the marines today grew up with TV, videogames, and computers. So we thought, how can we educate them, how can we engage them and make them want to learn? This is perfect.'*[7]

In this way, since the 1980s, the American defence forces have approached the commercial games industry to get them to create simulations that give soldiers the feeling of operating in a 'real' war. To an ever-increasing extent, the American army has applied war games to train its soldiers. Occasionally the training is limited to shooting with guns and riding in tanks, but sometimes the games offer large-scale virtual environments in which various war activities can be practised. Because the software of the games can be adapted in all kinds of ways, and because experiences during the game approach those in reality, games offer a suitable medium *par excellence* for the training activities.

PLAYING WITH DEADLY PRECISION

In order to prepare soldiers for 'objective' reality, the technology of the video game has been comprehensively adopted into army practice. Nevertheless, this does not offer a satisfactory answer to the question as to whether or not and how individual players from various countries identify with the soldier role. In order to elucidate this aspect, the concept of technology must be taken in a wider sense. Technology covers the way in which social reality is experienced. After all, technology is not neutral. It comprises an implicit picture of human self-understanding. This is also evident in the third development in the co-operation between the military forces and the games industry: the fusion of war images with the special effects from video games.

While existing pictures from the war in Afghanistan, Iraq and Somalia are being adopted into video games, advertisements to encourage recruitment into the American army occasionally make use of digital images from video games. The game called *Delta Force: Black Hawk Down* (NovaLogic, 2003) contains processed film and television images of the struggle in Mogadishu, the capital of Somalia.[8] The game *Close Combat: First to Fight* (2005) issued by the American publisher Global Star goes a step further. The characters from which a player can choose to bring a mission to a successful conclusion are marines who are still active in Iraq or have just returned from that country: the sergeants Rudy Lacroix, Michael Vaz, Hector Arellano, corporal Eddie Garcia, and first lieutenant Trustun Connor. It is remarkable that the similarity is not restricted to their names. In the game, the soldiers have also been given the faces of these real-life marines.

The technical images from video games provide a suggestion of objectivity. The setting of games appears to be completely faithful and true to life. In the first Gulf War, this aspect led to much confusion among the public that followed the war on television. During a press conference, General Norman Schwarzkopf attempted to put an end to this perplexity by remarking that this war was concerned with a different reality: 'This is not a video game.' According to Schwarzkopf, this was 'a real war'. Encouraged to do so by the government, other American military leaders also informed the public that the pictures displayed on television did not have their origins in a popular video game. Nevertheless, the confusion as to whether the pictures involved a real war or a game did not impede the manufacturer, Sony, from patenting the brand of 'shock and awe' for its new war games. This war tactic had been deployed to paralyse the Iraqi army by means of a wave of heavy air attacks during the second Gulf War.

[26]

The extent to which the virtual world has penetrated everyday life is illustrated by the way in which soldiers who have grown up with video games experience 'objective' reality. To a new generation of national servicemen and women, video games have their own self-evidence or normality. Various interviews with soldiers indicate that they no longer distinguish between the physical and the mental sensations during a war and the experiences of violence during a game. Killing an enemy evokes increasingly fewer questions, it is experienced as being self-evident. In that respect, according to the twenty-five-year-old lieutenant and unit commander Nathaniel Fick, there is a difference between the war in Iraq and the Second World War: 'In World War Two, when the Marines hit the beaches, a surprisingly high percentage of them didn't fire their weapons. (...) Not these guys. (...) These guys have no problem with killing.'[9]

The way in which video games influence the experience of soldiers is also shown by the words of the nineteen-year-old American corporal Harold Tromble. When his unit landed in an Iraqi ambush, he could only think about his favourite video game Grand Theft Auto. He committed insubordination by contradicting the statement made by General Schwarzkopf that war is not a game: 'I was thinking *just one thing when we drove into that ambush ... "Grand Theft Auto: Vice City". I felt like I was living it when I seen the flames coming out of the windows, the blown-up car in the street, guys crawling around shooting at us. It was fucking cool.'* [10]

PUBLIC ENEMY NO. 1: THE THREAT TO THE CITY

It is clear that the virtual world of games cannot be reduced to trivial entertainment. In the standard work *Vom Kriege*, dating from 1831, the Prussian general and theorist Carl von Clausewitz stated that 'war is an extension of politics with different resources'. Nowadays, you may wonder if games are an extension of war by means of other resources. It is indisputable that video games possess a form of reality that cannot be dismissed as pure illusion. To an ever-increasing degree, these games are successful in getting the players to forget that there is some kind of machine between the player and everyday reality. To make the confusion complete, the American army had a Blackhawk helicopter circle above the conference centre during the largest meeting of gamers in Los Angeles in May 2003. American soldiers invaded the conference and replayed a scene from the game *America's Army*, in which an elite trooper who has landed behind enemy lines has to be rescued.

[27

The virtual world of video games and the 'objective' world are beginning to resemble one another to an increasing extent. War games give the players the impression that they are linked up to an 'objective' reality, and 'real' war situations give soldiers the idea that they have landed in a video game. In that respect, *Full Spectrum Warrior* is one of the most realistic representations of the current activities of the American army. That is no coincidence. *Full Spectrum Warrior* has travelled in the opposite direction from games such as *Army Battlezone* and *Marine Doom*. The game is a product of the American army. Originally, *Full Spectrum Warrior* was a simulation exercise that was used as training for a new form of war activity. This simulation enjoyed so much success among the soldiers that the army decided to introduce a commercial version on to the market. *'The game is the most realistic representation of Army doctrine I know of. Players will have to use the same tactics an Army squad actually uses in the field to capture terrain. These include things like suppressing, flanking and ambushing*,' narrates director Will Stahl of Pandemic Studios, responsible for the game.[11]

Full Spectrum Warrior breaks with the classic war activities in which a city, surrounded by stone walls with watchtowers is a difficult obstacle to the enemy forces. In *Full Spectrum Warrior* the fights in the capital of the country of Zekistan are concentrated in locations such as building blocks and the roofs of buildings The fight no longer takes place outside the centre but rather in the centre of the city, in the middle of densely populated areas. Enemies are no longer a danger to the nation but a danger to the city. The game shows that the distinction between the police force and the army has become a question of gradation. Previously, the police and the army concentrated on two different forms of security. The duties of the police were limited to the internal safety of the country whereas the army was outward-oriented and responsible for external security. Both organizations are now more intimately linked than ever before. To an ever-greater extent, the police are assuming military features and the army is being deployed to protect citizens within the country's own borders or those of another country.

28]

In the game, one player is chosen as the leader of an infantry unit. It is his or her duty to lead the unit across an urban war zone. He or she can choose one of two teams for this purpose: the Alpha or the Bravo team. The military action in the capital consists of person-to-person fighting and is referred to as MOUT (*Military Operations in Urban Terrain*). MOUT is a form of keeping order in a densely populated environment with many obstacles. Blocks, booby-traps, bombs, traffic congestion, ambushes, and snipers who can hit their target at a distance of six hundred metres are part of everyday reality here. Previously effective and trusted military tactics no longer work within this urban environment. According to General Norman Schwarz-kopf, those traditional tactics were based on the size of the armies and the power of the weapons: '*One of the standard rules of warfare is the attacker should outnumber the defender, a minimum of three to one and if it gets a strongly fortified position, five to one.*'[12] These tactics of capturing the public space of a city with much display of power are no longer effective in the twenty-first century. Various war games indicate that the power of large numbers is no longer a valid element. In an urban environment, the enemy can hide almost anywhere. He can open fire from any corner. Heavy air fire and the use of tanks, as in the game *Battlezone*, are no longer realistic. Those weapons have been definitively consigned to the history of war. According to the text on the official internet site of *Full Spectrum Warrior*, only small, lightly armed units are capable of restoring order to public space: *'Today's Army is discovering that the only way to effectively cleanse a city of its hostile elements is with the use of small, technologically superior squads of soldiers that excel in block-to-block combat. This method is much more dangerous for the invader, however, and requires highly trained and well-coordinated teams of individual soldiers.'*

For this reason, players are trained in fights from 'block-to-block', in which the emphasis is placed on the shooting skills of the individual players to a lesser degree. Whereas old games focus on shooting with weapons and riding in tanks, soldiers are now taught to operate in teams. Technology that enables the players to communicate immediately with one another is an essential part of this new dynamics. The position and actions of the players are consistently based on up-to-date information. Extensive communication possibilities enable a team to react immediately. With the advent of this interactive element in games warfare, a point has been reached at which everything depends on the mutual relationships of the members and the co-ordination of the team. No longer is the information subordinate to the operation, as in *Kriegsspiel* in which the leaders of the army waited until sufficient data were available for successful action. There is now mention of a series of actions that have a direct influence on the mutual relationships within the team. In that circuit of mutual relationships, the operation and the information constantly influence one another. During the operation, information is obtained that immediately gives guidance and direction to the soldiers of the military unit.

[29

A NEW GAME DISCIPLINE

What are the consequences of the fusion of the virtual environment of games with the many aspects of warfare and our 'objective' reality? In order to examine the mechanisms that generate a military experience, it is necessary to look at the criticism of current games. A large part of this criticism is already widely known. It is oriented toward the issue of whether or not violence in games is as innocent as is alleged. Scientists are still divided as to whether or not there is a causal link between the behaviour of young people and violence in the media. A more important aspect for obtaining a satisfactory answer to questions concerning which processes play a role in the transformation of self-experience is the American army's criticism of the most recent war games and the consequences of this remarkable criticism. In the army's view, games ought to take into consideration the new circumstances in which soldiers have to operate. Although it may sound rather improbable, the complaint is that video games show too much war. A player encounters more enemies than in a normal war situation. Moreover, a player shoots too often and has to make use of too many different weapons. For these reasons, the American army believes that more emphasis ought to be placed on the context. War games should take into account the norms and values, the traditions and beliefs of the people who live in the areas in which the soldiers are active. In short, a new generation of soldiers and players ought to display empathy, be able to communicate with the population, and be aware of the beliefs of the local residents.

30]

One thing is clear: in order to function as a fully-fledged military subject in an existing environment, further discipline is necessary. *Full Spectrum Warrior* and *America's Army* are the first games that meet the complaints of the American army that weapons cannot be used without rules. Correctional techniques are used in these games and the players have to adhere to well-defined regulations and norms. These are internalized by obliging the players to follow various training courses. Before new players can begin to play *America's Army* on the internet, they have to perform specific exercises that teach them to cope with various weapons. But the training does not remain restricted to the use of weapons and military tactics. A player also gains medical knowledge that can be used if another player gets injured or wounded. Due to the intensive training, the players are drilled, as it were, to function in an optimum manner as fully-fledged elite troops in an urban environment. Their virtual constitution is aligned to the role they play in the military unit and to the nature of the urban zone in which the unit is active.

In his work *Surveiller et punir* (Discipline and Punish), the French philosopher Michel Foucault demonstrates that these ideas concerning discipline, which developed in the eighteenth century in sciences structured around the 'police' – the guardians of the modern *polis* – are not as innocent as they appear. According to Foucault, a disciplinary society assumes a completely different attitude to the body than the sovereign society that preceded it. In the disciplinary society, the idea arose that the individual is a changeable entity. In army practice, the consequences of this are immediately visible. In the seventeenth century, the soldier was described as someone who was recognizable due to his courage or desire to fight. But that changed from the eighteenth century onward. Based on the humanist insight of the Enlightenment, various practices were applied in the army to instil the required behaviour. From a meaningful body that radiates energy and honour, the body of a soldier was slowly reduced to a cog in the machinery. The soldier was formed by training in which he learned to keep his head erect, his back straight, and to move in a uniform manner. With the aid of correctional exercise, aimed at realizing specific and measurable effects, the soldier was furnished with a coherent identity. Disciplining did not only take place in army camps. The discipline-oriented techniques were also deployed in other social institutions: prison, hospital, school, and at work. Due to the fact that insights from the social sciences were systematically applied in these institutions – Foucault refers to them as 'disciplinary practices' – they produced specific subjects.

[31

The disciplining techniques in which the body of the player is both the object of analysis and the goal of power are deliberately deployed in *America's Army*. In order to play *America's Army* on internet as a new player, one first has to register. After the registration has been completed, the player undergoes comprehensive training in which he or she acquires the skills that are needed to function in an optimum way in the national army. The training programme consists of four components: Rifle Range, Obstacle Course, US Weapons, and Tactical Training. In these components, the gamer learns the significance of the various signals given by other players in the game. Every part of the training must be successfully completed before the trainee can progress to the next exercise. Only those who score well in the training may continue the course.

The exercises are held in the open range of Fort Benning in Georgia, a location used by the real American army. In the rifle-range training, players must be able to use an M-16 weapon to hit targets at distances of between 30 and 300 metres. In the definitive test, players are given forty bullets with which they, from a standing or reclining position, have to hit targets that suddenly jump up. They have to hit a minimum of 23 targets in order to progress. If they succeed, this represents a satisfactory completion of their training and they may call themselves *Marksman*. *Sharpshooters* are able to hit 30 targets while *Experts* hit 36. Only the players who reach the status of *Expert* are allowed admission into the *Sniper School* in the first part of *America's Army*. There, the *Experts* are taught to handle M-24 and M-82 snipers' weapons. Accordingly, discipline among the players is gradually enforced by means of repetitive training. They are not only subjected to the discipline of the army, the players also learn to identify with the regulations that apply in the army.

IF YOU PLAY TOO LONG, YOU START SEEING THINGS

The producers of *America's Army* emphasize that the game is a *'realistic representation of the values, units, the material and the career opportunities that make the American army the best army in the world'*. The game has become an important component of the communications strategy of the American army to allow young people to become familiar with the ideas and role of the national army. According to a spokesperson, it shows young people that the army commits itself to fighting terrorist forces who aim at attacking the United States and the freedom of its population at various fronts all over the world. During the various parts of the game, players are given biographic sketches of real soldiers in the American army. In doing so, *America's Army* wishes to allow them to experience how soldiers prepare themselves to defend freedom. *'It's a much more efficient and effective vehicle for the Army to provide information to young people than the other media we use,'* explains Chris Chambers in an interview.[13]

The influence of the army permeates everyday life down to the finest details. It has penetrated the popular culture of games, it structures the experience of many players, and determines to a certain extent the way in which they perceive themselves. Despite the many correspondences between the different war games and 'objective' reality, there is always one important difference. It seems as if everything in virtual reality is authorized in the struggle to restore and maintain law and order. Are the legal norms, which have been established in international treaties and agreements such as the Geneva Convention, applicable in virtual space? At first sight every legal norm seems

32]

to have disappeared. The fights in war games are not stopped in order to reach a peaceful solution on which both parties can agree. Players have the latest automatic weapons at their disposal, there is no shortage of ammunition, there are no negotiations between the opposing parties, and an enemy is seldom overcome and taken prisoner. In simple terms: standing in the way means being shot down.

But is there truly mention of an exceptional situation or norm-free environment in games such as *America's Army* and *Full Spectrum Warrior*, of a laissez-faire zone in which no legal norms whatsoever are applicable or can be imposed? In order to respond to that question, we have to look at the system of rules and sanctions that apply to all players. In games such as *Full Spectrum Warrior*, the protection of the national state has made way for the military maintenance of public order. This transition is not restricted to an arsenal of new tactics and strategies that distinguish themselves from warfare as we used to know it. It is no longer sufficient to ascertain that the commitment of the army has changed. The shift from protecting national security to the maintenance of public order also brings changes in other areas. What we see in video games is a different concept of security, one that is supported by a system of detailed rules and sanctions. A short history of the punishment applied will put this regime in a wider perspective.

[33

Changes in the shape of society are linked to other notions of punishment. In the sovereign society, absolute power was in the hands of the monarch. A breach of the law was regarded as an attack on his person. *'In every offence there was a crimen majestatis and in the least criminal a potential regicide,'* writes Michel Foucault in *Surveiller et punir*.[14] Under the keen eye of the monarch and his subjects, public punishment was carried out to expose the truth by means of corporal punishment on the scaffold. It was not justice or prevention but taking revenge for the tarnished honour of the sovereign that formed the objective of the punishment. This punishment varied from the application of a brand mark – a letter was stamped on the shoulder of the guilty person by means of a red-hot iron – to the public lashing of the criminal by a functionary with a bullwhip. Another variant was that the criminal was tied up on the scaffold with a board on his body telling what he had done. Usually, that kind of spectacle lasted around one hour.

With the shift from the sovereign form of state to a disciplinary form of state, the punishment no longer concentrated on the body of the criminal but rather on the soul of the guilty party. The punishment developed into the most hidden part of the punishment process, as Foucault put it. It was no longer carried out in public but behind the walls of closed and secluded institutions. Furthermore, this had the aim of realizing specific and measurable effects on the guilty person. The issue of whether one was guilty or not guilty no longer seemed sufficient. New questions concerning the truth were posed: 'What is the underlying cause of the crime? How did the criminal get this far? In which way could he function normally in society again?' In order to respond to these questions, a legal punishment process was constructed in which social sciences such as psychology and sociology played a major role. Under the influence of these sciences, the criminal became an object of knowledge and power. And although people at the beginning of the nineteenth century still regarded prison as a new institute, its disciplinary working turned out to be similar to that of a range of other institutions with which an individual was confronted during his or her life: family, school, army, factory, hospital, etc. The individual consistently begins anew. At school they say that you are not at home. At work they say: 'You are no longer at school.'

NOT SCHOOLS BUT NEW PRISONS

At this moment, we are at a point where the disciplinary society is slowly shifting toward an organizational form that is also referred to as the 'the control society'. According to the French philosopher Gilles Deleuze, we have passed the expiry date of the institutions of the disciplinary society.[15] There is a general crisis in the field of every form of custody. The walls of closed institutions are being demolished, as it were. The consequences of the changes are visible in all kinds of practices, such as prison, hospital, school, and the working environment. Isn't electronic supervision, where the detainee undergoes his or her punishment outside the prison walls, a perfect example of the virtualization of prison? By means of domestic care, another institution, the hospital, relocates its activities to the living environment of the patient. The transition from school to work has also become diffuse. At work, one has to undergo regular refresher courses to keep one's knowledge up to date. At the same time, one also takes a laptop home so that one can work at the weekend. But this alteration in structure is most prominent in a series of changes that is characteristic of the current pursuit of absolute safety in society. The new way in which the regulations are maintained and the deployment of new techniques to prevent any disturbance of public order are perfect examples of this culture of control.

It is the great merit of the sociologist David Garland that he has demonstrated that the culture of control ought to be regarded as an abrupt and clear break with what is called *'penal welfarism'* in criminology. In his book entitled *The Culture of Control*, Garland observes that penal welfarism originated around the end of the nineteenth century and thrived between 1950 and 1960.[16] The major concept of penal welfarism is that the legal code must protect citizens against the unbridled power of the government. Even more essential than this critical function in relation to the power of the government is the importance that is attached to the resocialization of the criminal. The attention of various professional organizations is oriented toward the psychopathic aspects of the criminal on the one hand and toward the social and economic causes of crime on the other. As a result, relatively little attention is paid to the victim. In this vision, crime issues from the impropriety of individuals and families, it arises from social arrears in the form of poor economic circumstances, or is the result of insufficient access to the labour market.

[35

Since the seventies, the judicial climate in Europe and the United States has been changing radically. Although penal welfarism has worked relatively satisfactorily for almost a hundred years, the judicial system is less and less oriented toward protecting citizens against the power of the government and is increasingly oriented toward preventing crime and reducing anxiety about crime. Interest in the delinquent or criminal character of the transgressor has faded into the background, the symbolic figure of the victim has become the political imperative. *'Victims must be protected, their voices must be heard, their memory honoured, their anger expressed, their fears addressed'*, is Garland's conclusion.[17]

According to Garland, social, economic, cultural and political changes play a major role in the sudden reversal of these two approaches – penal welfarism and the culture of control. The prevailing political philosophy in the Western world has changed. Social democracy has made way for a combination of neo-liberalism that is oriented toward market working, privatization and entrepreneurship, and neo-conservatism that places the emphasis on the exceptional position of the family and the role of the national state. In addition, the increased significance of the mass media, such as television, and the proliferation of the car, which has allowed people to live at a greater distance from their work and settle on the edge of the city, for example, have contributed to the fact that a new 'ideological environment' has arisen in which the old adage of penal welfarism – 'not prisons but schools' – has been completely reversed.

WE KILL ACCORDING TO STRICT RULES

In a culture of control, new technologies are deployed as a strategy to make criminal behaviour practically impossible or to prevent a breach of public order. We also see this in the war games world. Let us take the virtual space of *America's Army* as our starting point. Which regime of rules and sanctions, which applies to all players, is valid in this video game? And, are these rules and sanctions a herald of a juridical arsenal of techniques that will also have an effect upon our physical world? In order to come to a good understanding of the specific regime of rules and sanctions in games, one must realize that the virtual world is not an autonomous free state. The words of lieutenant colonel E. Casey Wardynski – director of the Army's Office of Economic and Manpower Analysis – indicate that detailed rules have been set down for the *America's Army* game: '*The military kills people, but you need to understand we do it in strict guidelines. This isn't Attila the Hun's Army. There is no Deathmatch free-for-all mode of play in America's Army. If you play our game, we expect you to act like a soldier performing the tasks that soldiers do. Those who repeatedly can't will be banned.*' [18]

All players are expected to know a uniform system of rules and regulations, known as the '*Rules of Engagement*' (ROE). The *Rules of Engagement* are based on a system of honour that is expressed in points. The number of points that players gain forms the most important criterion by which they can distinguish themselves from other players. For example, all players receive ten points when starting the game. After every training session or action session, their achievements are registered and stored in a personal report. At the moment someone excels in a feature, he or she is allocated a higher status in the team.

36]

The higher one's status, the more say he or she has in the team and the more important his or her role is in the operation. In many ways, these games respect the most important rules of the American army. First of all, team members who have been wounded must be brought to safety so that they can be given medical assistance. In addition, not all the points are assigned to the player who is the best sniper. The team game, the defence, staying alive, and supporting the other elite soldiers in the team are all rewarded with points. The team interest is also a feature of the *Counterstrike* game. In this game, players choose to be a part of a specialist team that liberates hostages and defuses bombs, or they can choose the side of the terrorist group that carries out assaults and eliminates anti-terrorist units. Without assistance from their team-mates, individual players in *Counterstrike* have no chance of survival whatsoever. It is not without reason that the most important tactic in this game is: '*Check Position. Follow Your Friend.*'

The system of allocating points to all kinds of behaviour and to a player's commitment functions in two ways. Besides being a collection of regulations, this regime is also used to prohibit some actions. What is apparently pure entertainment and also a free play of forces is actually a specific system of precisely defined rules and sanctions. It is no coincidence that the list of prohibited actions which lead to a deduction of points is borrowed from those of the American army. This includes the shooting of innocent citizens, obstructing fellow team members, and damaging objects that are supposed to be protected. These violations are carefully registered in the personal dossiers of the players.

If players violate the *Rules of Engagement* by hitting other team members or refusing to work together, points are deducted from their personal score of honour. The regime concludes with a punishment that is imposed if players have broken the *Rules of Engagement* several times. If this is the case, they are sent to a virtual representation of an existing American prison: the United States Military Prison in Ft. Leavenworth, Kansas. But the rules in *America's Army* are not only enforced by deducting points from the personal scores of the players or by having players spend playing time in the Ft. Leavenworth prison. If a rule has been ignored too often, the ultimate sanction is imposed. The players' access to the official game server is temporarily blocked. In cases of repetition, players are banned from the official server that is needed to gain access to the game on internet. Can we observe that players are thus gradually taught to behave positively? In any case, the rules and sanctions seem to determine their self-experience just as forcefully as the training to which they were subjected.

GAME OVER: TWO LIVES LEFT

The practice of the *Rules of Engagement* is optimized by means of a technically refined system. In order to have the entire body of rules and sanctions function properly, the supervision depends on a permanent and all-embracing registration. The virtual control, which covers all players and is oriented to all their actions, is unlimited. But, apart from their symbolic significance, do the various actions in video games actually have an effect on the behaviour of the players? Many players experience the sanctions as trivial. After all, it is possible to log in on the server under another name. But the consequence of this is that the players cannot take their scores of honour with them. As a result, they have to begin again with a low score and have less chance of being invited by other players to play the game online. This is outlined as follows on the website of *America's Army*: *'The game establishes a "records jacket" for each player, as much as the army has a personnel record for each soldier. In this record, filed under the player's nom de guerre, will be the player's training and service record to include acts of fratricide, violations of Rules of Engagement and other information that attests to a game player's performance as a member of a team. Other team players will be less likely to choose you as a team-mate if you have a history of friendly-fire violations or low standing in honour points. In addition a combat effectiveness meter gauges the player's ability to hit the target in different situations and also how responsible the player is in combat. This too will affect a player's ranking.'*

The system within which players are valued, ranked and divided by means of points is being applied on internet to an ever-increasing degree. The international trading site *eBay* makes use of a similar system to regulate the buying and selling of articles. For a long a time, an auction was a local event that took place according to local customs. The principle of the garage sale and the flea market is simple. The buyer and seller meet one another and negotiate there and then about the goods. The rule of 'money back if dissatisfied' works well because the buyer knows where the seller lives. But the internet is boundless and the scope of the auction has been extended accordingly. Internet offers

38]

everyone the opportunity to log in on a virtual auction. It is no longer necessary for both parties and the goods to be situated at one spot.

This new way of buying and selling goods brought many problems in the initial stages. The anonymity of the participants made it difficult to establish the reliability of the participating trading partners. Even if the trading partner was regarded as being fair, one could not be sure that he or she was actually who he or she pretended to be. To solve this problem, eBay introduced a valuation system in which both the buyer and the seller have enough information to decide whether or not they wish to do business with one another. Every eBay member has a feedback profile. This profile consists of a score, plus comments from other members who have bought something from, or sold something to, this person. With ten positive remarks, the eBay member is assigned a yellow star; with fifty, they get a dark-blue star, etc. A red star is the ultimate reward and is assigned if a member receives 100,000 positive remarks. In this way, only reliable parties survive. [39

Where is this perspective leading us in our 'objective' reality? Do we see certain facets from virtual reality recurring in physical reality? When we translate the regime applied in games to 'true' reality, this irrevocably leads to the conclusion that individuals are no longer born with unalienable and fundamental rights. Several weeks after the terrorist bombing of 7/7/2005 in the London underground, in which 52 people lost their lives, Tony Blair made this clear. He announced that the United Kingdom would no longer adhere to the European Charter of Human Rights. The European Charter brings together the civil, political, social and economic rights under six themes: dignity, freedom, equality, solidarity, civility, and justice. After the announcement of the Prime Minister, Lord Falconer – the minister who shares the Justice portfolio and is also head of the British legal system – reinforced this attitude by saying that human rights should not prevail above the safety of British citizens. In other words, the tights of the suspects should not prevail above those of the possible victims among the British population.

When we allow these statements by Blair and Falconer to sink in, this leads to the unsettling observation that we are no longer born with fundamental and inalienable rights such as the right to equal protection by the law or the right to be declared innocent until the contrary has been proved in a public sitting. By acting in a certain way, by displaying 'good' behaviour, we must now earn the most important rights which issued from the British *Bill of Rights* of 1689, the

American Constitution of 1787, and the French *Déclaration des droits de l'homme et du citoyen* of 1789, and those compiled by the United Nations in 1948 in the *Universal Declaration of Human Rights*. This is the way we should interpret the statement of the Dutch Minister of Health who, in an interview over people who 'lived unhealthily' remarked: '*There is no such thing as a right to live unhealthily.*' [19]

Instead of people being born with inalienable rights, a system of penalty points has arisen that is linked to all kinds of stipulations that increasingly legally differentiate the behaviour of individuals. Is this a different substantiation of liability and accountability? Let us limit ourselves to several examples of this new way of guiding people's lives. Isn't it a coincidence that an increasing number of countries are introducing a points system for the driving licence in order to reduce the number of traffic accidents and to combat the risks of drink and drugs in traffic? There is not only a fine for driving too fast or driving under the influence of drink, the offender is also given penalty points. Once the limit has been reached, the driving licence is suspended and, with this, access to physical networks such as motorways is terminated. Game Over! And what is the difference between the American notion of '*three strikes and you're out,*' which means that a third conviction automatically leads to a long prison sentence regardless of the nature of the violation, and the virtual reality of the gamer? Is the notion of '*three strikes, you're out*' not the ultimate games perspective of the gamer? Finally, in countries such as the USA and the UK, there is a system that gives asylum seekers points on the basis of their qualifications, skills and working history. The more points an asylum seeker has, the greater the chance of a residence permit. In short, the strategy of awarding points makes it possible to manage and control people more and more. They are precision-guided by a detailed points system. People still wish to use the rod to influence people's souls but this currently takes place in a more subtle manner than in the disciplinary society. In a culture of control, everything depends on an endless system of punishment and reward.

40]

THE ARCHITECTURE OF CONTROL FREAKS

Until now, the analysis of the militarization of life was oriented toward the forming of a military experience among players and the advent of rules and sanctions that are based on detailed points systems. But how does this self-experience manifest itself in our physical environment and how are those rules and sanctions implemented there? In other words, which physical echoes does this virtual reality generate in 'objective' reality? It is only a small step to link the militarization of life to a form of architecture that has been thrown across the city like a military control net whose mesh is being drawn increasingly tight. This architecture not only contributes to a specific self-experience but also leads to a different partitioning of physical space. This development is already visible in London, where, under the guise of accessibility and liveability, a car-deterrent system that controls and registers the place, time and patterns of people in public space has been installed. A cordon of cameras has been erected around 21 km² in the centre of the city, with the aim of reducing the traffic congestion. The cameras are linked to a computer system that recognizes the number plates of the cars. As soon as car drivers enter the area between seven in the morning and six in the evening on working days, they have to pay a toll. If that sum is not paid before twelve o'clock on the same day, they will be fined.

[41

In his books *City of Quartz* and *Ecology of Fear*, Mike Davis describes the consequences of the militarization of life for public space in Los Angeles. Since the riots of 1992, there has been an increasing recession and a flight of capital from the city. Harsh cutbacks have been introduced, an astonishing number of murders have been committed (despite the ceasefire between the gangs), and the arms trade in the suburbs has expanded dramatically. These developments have led to a social schism that is articulated architectonically in a series of exterior spaces – shopping malls, gated communities, amusement parks, Business Improvement Districts (BIDs) – that are protected and isolated. City Walk in downtown Los Angeles is one of the most renowned expressions of this trend. The complex has been built around the idea of the American 'main street' and reaches back to the era in which cars were only a sporadic occurrence and citizens could participate light-heartedly in public life in the city. A broad shopping street, designed by the American office The Jerde Partnership, is situated in the midst of an area that is surrounded by buildings where visitors have to park their cars. Not only are all the entrances to the obligatory car parks monitored with cameras, the parking charges must also be paid in advance. Homeless people and beggars are refused entrance to this closed-off area by the security services in attendance.

To allow the spatial and social apartheid to function, the physical space is endowed with an architecture that is subject to permanent supervision. At present, the perception system of an average office block makes use of panoptical images, changes in smell, temperature and humidity, motion detection, and occasionally also audio signals.[20] But Davis observes that, for security reasons, buildings are also equipped with aggression detectors, programs for detection and recognition, and facial recognition systems. These technologies, which are linked to computer networks, are used to monitor the behaviour of the visitors. The distinction between architecture and the maintenance of public order is disappearing. Ultimately the interaction between architecture and life will lead to the unique point at which the city will transform into a military fort or, as the Italian philosopher Giorgio Agamben claims in his *Homo Sacer* cycle, into a camp. In that case, every object is equipped with monitoring devices connected by networks. In this wireless Global Information Grid, or GIG city, the spaces are dimensions with many entrances and exits, which do not allow themselves to be defined by fixed systems of points and positions. They are unstable, make connections with other spaces, disappear, or are adopted into other environments. The difference between interior and exterior has become gradual. A new interior and exterior is consistently being generated in the urban space.[21]

At the end of this development, the architecture of the urban space will no longer be defined by the separate physical shells of the most important social institutions of modernity: schools, factories, prisons, hospitals. The spaces of the disciplinary society, assigned to their specific function, will have made way for the slick, encapsulated interior spaces of the control society. These pseudo-isolated or encapsulated spaces will contain shopping areas combined with offices, apartments, schools, and hotels. Because the space has been condensed, the residents no longer need to go out. A new spatial entity that we refer to as an 'Urban Container' will be created. The Urban Container forms a designated area in an urban landscape in which various activities are concentrated. This model is already unmistakably permeating the urban landscape. In areas with high population density, such as Singapore, Hong Kong and Tokyo, giant complexes that combine functions are being built on metro and train stations. In the USA, such complex-

42]

es are being linked to motorways and car parks. In European cities, too, the conjunction of various social institutions can also be found. For example the TGV station *Le Triangle des Gares* in the French city of Lille accommodates a shopping centre, apartment blocks, a school, a hotel, and office complexes.

Several significant questions arise from the perspective of the Urban Container. Which developments have contributed to the fact that the Container has become the most important architecture of a culture of control? Can the boundaries of the semi-public space of the Container be rapidly and flexibly constructed, just like the environments in the games described? In which ways are the actions of people who live in the Container or remain there temporarily registered and updated? If we can obtain answers to these questions, we will know if the installation of the regime of military rules and sanctions from the games of *America's Army* and *Full Spectrum Warrior* has been absorbed into the architecture of life. Game On?

[43

CHAPTER 2

The Architecture
of the Urban Container

THe conclusion of the previous chapter was that life in the city is beginning to take on an increasing number of military features. This does not mean that military techniques completely control and run our daily lives. Life repeatedly manages to escape from these. The militarization of life reveals itself where a culture of control is given shape.

The culture of control makes use of detailed points systems that aim to ensure that we adhere to the precisely described rules. In addition, we are no longer born with inalienable and fundamental rights but we accumulate these over a lifespan by performing the right actions or avoiding bad ones. Finally, we are trained to function in a military 'urban setting' in which bounded interior spaces ensure a permanent form of enclosure and exclusion. The encapsulating architecture that is the result of this forms the model for the current culture of control, with the Urban Container as the most articulate example.

What are the origins of the Urban Container? The Urban Container was created at the moment when social institutions no longer had their own delineated spaces, as in the disciplinary society, but were absorbed into a larger physical entity in which diverse functions such as shopping, living, working and education were all allocated a place. 'Container' comes from the Latin word *continere*, which is a combination of the words *com* (together) and *tenere* (to hold). This is what these large-scale complex do: enclose and keep together. In the Urban Container, the major social institutions of modernity – offices, schools, prisons, hospitals, shopping centres – have been turned inside out and pressed into one architectonic space. Just as in the shipping trade, the Urban Container stands for standardization and optimization of the available space. The economic credo applies here: *'Small space, fewer costs.'*

The prefix 'Urban' is no coincidence. Although it is difficult to specify the place and time of the first Urban Containers, a historical parallel can be given. The modern Container displays many correspondences with the medieval walled town. Here, too, there was a tendency to seek protection and to exclude undesired persons. For a long time the walled town was an example of the way in which large communities could be accommodated in a bounded space within which the world could unfold. In the medieval model, the town and the countryside can be easily located. They are often clearly delineated places with their own specific physical, social and symbolic characteristics. However, with the new geography, an end has gradually come to the clear demarcation between wild nature and stylized human culture: the transition from the 'interior' of the demarcated urban culture to the 'exterior' of wild nature has vanished.

[45

A significant development that lies at the basis of the disappearance of this distinction between the city and the country is the increased urbanity of our living environment. We have become urban creatures. Whereas there were eleven cities with more than a million residents in 1900, there are more than a hundred cities with more than three million residents at the beginning of the twenty-first century. Thirty-six cities even have more than eight million residents. Within twenty years, more than 90% of the world population will live in cities or urban areas. The strict division between the city and the countryside has vanished, dual categories such as 'centre' versus 'periphery' and 'nature' versus 'city' have thus become obsolete. For an adequate analysis of the spatial differentiations in our present-day landscape, we can no longer take the distinction between the countryside and the town as our most important reference point. We require other terms to delineate the concentration of collective activities and the redivision of boundaries.

As a result of the global developments sketched above – with the modern city as an expression of our society – we do not wish to treat the Urban Container as a historical phenomenon or urban artefact. Even if the idea of a sealed-off interior world, where functions like living, working and recreation converge on a limited surface area, can be recognized in various forms – the medieval city is only one manifestation of this – we nonetheless regard the encapsulated, multifunctional interior space of the Container as an architecture that is strongly related to the current culture of control. Our hypothesis that the Urban Container is the dominant urban typology of the culture of control not only says something about the nature of that culture but also entails that a new relationship between life and architecture is arising. What is the relationship between architecture and life when our lives are given shape in the interaction with a built environment whose aim is to rebuff people who are a threat to our security? On the basis of this question, in which architecture is regarded as a deadly weapon of enclosure and exclusion, we shall describe three typologies of the Urban Container: the *company town*, the compound, and the *E-City*. These typologies can easily be dismissed as modern or Utopian projects. However, the main issue is that of how the principles of the Container influence our present society.

46]

MATRUSHKA ARCHITECTURE: CITIES WITHIN A CITY

When dealing with the genealogy of the Urban Container, besides a description of the various typologies of enclosure and exclusion, attention must also be devoted to the most important social developments that have given rise to the culture of control. How did this perspective of combining the most complex and divergent functions manage to gain dominance? And how has it been able to develop into a broad movement in which safe and controlled interior worlds are being created while the exterior world has been defined as dangerous and the *'the over the wall crowd'* may in no way whatsoever enter the sphere of the Urban Container?

Under the pressure of increased land prices, the congestion of the inner cities, and the new regulations, a new type of building, in which several functions were combined, arose in downtown Chicago and New York at the end of the nineteenth century. The most renowned example of this kind of city within a city is the 1890 Auditorium Building by Adler and Sullivan in Chicago. The complex accommodates an auditorium for 4200 visitors, a hotel with 400 rooms, and 136 offices. After the success of the Auditorium Building, an increasing number of complexes were built to combine various functions. In Miami, the town hall was combined with a prison and a court of law. The New York Hospital coupled apartments, gyms and lounges to its hospital programme. But the best example of this new kind of building is situated in Chicago, where the church spire of the First United Methodist Church is located on the twenty-first storey. The second storey accommodates the Dixon Chapel, the marriage room, and the offices of the church. There are classrooms on the third and fourth floors, a childcare centre, a conference hall, and a choir room. The fifth to the twentieth floors have been hired out as office space, primarily to lawyers' offices that regard the situation near the most important government buildings as a major advantage.

Another impulse toward the current Urban Containers can be found in the Rockefeller Center in New York. The need for a new opera house formed the initiative for one of the largest buildings in this metropolis. The quest for a suitable site for the music hall resulted in an enormous complex of several buildings between 48th and 51st Street, and Fifth Avenue and the Avenue of the Americas. Between 1931 and 1939, fourteen buildings arose here. The Time-Life building, dating from 1961, is the most recent addition to this complex. Besides offices, shops, restaurants, exhibition areas, film and television studios, the buildings contain the Radio City Music Hall with almost 6,000 seats. The Rockefeller Center is situated at a metro stop, which, with a comprehensive shopping mall, makes it a part of the enormous complex. One of the most striking features of the Center is that the exterior of the sizeable complex gives no indication of the diversity inside.

With the proliferation of the car and the extensive network of motorways, an increasing number of people in the United States began to take up residence at some distance from their work, settling on the edge of town. Ghettos arose in the inner cities, clusters of poor families lived in areas where there were almost no public facilities or social amenities such as shops, transport and work. Because people were exchanging the inner city of Chicago for a house in the suburbs, fewer people were needed for the maintenance and supervision of the buildings. In this way, the lack of occupancy contributed to the unemployment of caretakers. In 1955, confronted by the decreasing numbers of members of his trade union, the chairman of the International Union of Building Maintenance Employees, Bill McFetridge, asked the architect Bertrand Goldberg to design a building that 'could per-

[47

suade people to come back into town to live by showing them a desirable way of living in town' [22] The apartment complex that Goldberg created bears the name Marina City and consists of corn-cob-shaped cylindrical high-rise apartment blocks that are equipped with car parks for the residents. The high-rise blocks stand on a platform of buildings in which office areas, a hotel, a theatre and a restaurant are accommodated. In contrast to the structure of the Rockefeller Center, Goldberg did not have the intention of enriching the city with extensive public facilities. By creating a metropolitan environment in a relatively autonomous inner world, he wanted to offer a new alternative to people who had left the inner city of Chicago: *'In order to induce people to live downtown, I had to have an exciting environment – a total environment.'* [23] The billboard adjoining the building site displayed the stirring slogan: *'City within a City'*.

48]   At the end of the Second World War, the French architect Le Corbusier introduced various spatial concepts that bore similarities to these American examples. In the assignment from the French Ministry for Post-war Reconstruction, he developed a large-scale apartment block that he called the *'unité d'habitation de grandeur conforme'*.[24] The prototype is a model that offers accommodation to 1600 people. With this number, Le Corbusier deliberately sought alignment with nineteenth-century ideas on living communities. More than one hundred years earlier, the French Utopian socialist Charles Fourier had mentioned that number as the population of the living community of the *phalanstère*. The *phalanstère* – Fourier's alternative to a city and village – was an independent community that had to consist of 1620 members: 810 women and 810 men. In the *Communist Manifesto*, Karl Marx and Friedrich Engels sharply criticized the Utopian socialism of people such as Charles Fourier and Robert Owen: *'They still dream of experimental realization of their social Utopias, of founding isolated "phalansteres", of establishing "Home Colonies", or setting up a "Little Icaria" – duodecimo editions of the New Jerusalem – and to realize all these castles in the air, they are compelled to appeal to the feelings and purses of the bourgeois.'* But Le Corbusier unmistakably took into consideration the same ideal community as Fourier: a community that could function in relative isolation and independent of the direct environment.

In 1946, Le Corbusier was asked to realize his prototype in Marseilles in the surroundings of the Boulevard Michelet. He designed his own *phalanstère* there in the form of a cruise ship. To Le Corbusier, the cruise ship was the embodiment of the unprecedented possibility of an ideal, communal 'living machine'.[25] Eventually, the design bearing the name *Unité d'Habitation* was 138 metres long, 25 metres wide, and 56 metres tall. The rough block of concrete offers space to around 1200 people and is elevated from the ground by means of 34 columns. In order to graft the architecture onto life as much as possible, all kinds of facilities were realized for the residents. For example, a supermarket, a hairdresser's, a pharmacy, a post office, and a hotel are situated on the internal passageways of the seventh and eighth floors. There is a playground, an infant school, a sports hall, a theatre, and a 300-metres athletic track on the roof.

A year after the opening in 1952, at the ninth meeting of the *Congrès International d'Architecture Moderne* (CIAM), Le Corbusier invited his colleagues to become familiar with his all-embracing living machine. To underline the multiform nature of the complex, Le Corbusier asked Yannis Xenakis to organize a *'spatialized concert'*. The [49 Greek composer and architect Xenakis had four kinds of music played at various places on the roof: concrete music, traditional music from India and Japan, and jazz. As the highlight, a striptease act was carried out. Never before had the rules that had been formulated by this same Le Corbusier at the fourth CIAM congress in 1933 been so ignored. At this, the dogmatic Dutch congress participants left the meeting deeply shocked. Nineteen years previously, it had been agreed that the poor, often unhygienic living conditions in the large cities could be prevented by separating the functions of living, working, and recreation. But in 1952, Le Corbusier propagated the opposite: mono-functional areas in which people only lived or worked no longer served as the starting point for the design of modern cities. With Le Corbusier's plea to replace uniform living estates (suburbs), business districts (downtowns), industrial areas, and recreation parks with complete interior worlds in which living, working and recreation converge, the first support base was established for what could be called a 'new architecture of life': the Urban Container.

THE MULTINATIONALIZATION OF SPACE

A second social development to which the upsurge of the Urban Container can be related is the colonization of enormous pieces of land by wealthy companies. From the second half of the nineteenth century onward, large industrial enterprises who were active in the mining, steel, car and wood industries bought large areas around their factories.[26] Looking for suitable accommodation for their employees in the occasionally isolated areas where the raw materials were found, these enterprises created living areas in the vicinity in order to accommodate their employees. In this way, they prevented slums without facilities such as running water and sewerage arising around the company premises. Such slums gave the companies a bad name and generated undesired publicity. In addition, the unhygienic circumstances is such neighbourhoods contributed to the poor health of the employees and thus to a reduction in productivity.

As the employees went searching for the highest possible wages and the best work and living circumstances for themselves and their families, the number of facilities in these large-scale living estates gradually increased and the so-called *company towns* arose, with facilities such as hospitals, shops, petrol stations, and places of entertainment. Well-furnished houses, public facilities such as parks, schools, libraries and meeting and party halls, as well as social programmes for the families, contributed to the workers having a more healthy life while increasing their productivity. Besides these concrete objectives, the company towns also ensured that the employees were pleased to remain in the service of the enterprise for a longer time.

The architecture of the company town does not differ much from that of the most important building in the complex: the factory. The design of the houses in which the families lived, the church in which people prayed, and the school in which the children were taught resembles that of the factory in many respects. The result was a privatized area with a configuration of similar complexes where the life of the worker was shaped by means of specific factors. Each resident of the company town borrowed his status from his function as a worker and was bound by contract to uphold the rules and regulations that applied within this relatively secluded institution. As such, the residents were a part of the social order that was formed by a unique combination of working routine, an isolated location, and the code of conduct drawn up by the company. This unique combination ensured that the entire behaviour of the residents of the company towns was controlled by their employer who was simultaneously their landlord, rubbish collector, policeman, and judge. A good example of this kind of company town is that which the *Pullman Palace Car Company* built just south of Chicago in 1880. Under the management of George Mortimer Pullman (1831-1897), the company produced luxury sleeping wagons (couchettes) that were even equipped with facilities such as a library, card tables, and a special customer service. Pullman acquired international fame when he founded a city covering 16 km² for 6,000 employees: *Pullman Town*. In order to keep this conglomeration of houses, a library, market squares, and churches under control, the residents, more than 12,000 strong, were subjected to the rules and norms of the Pullman company. From the prohibition of drinking alcohol to the place where the washing had to be hung out to dry, everything was equally meticulously elaborated and written down.[27] The way in which a worker articulated life in the complex interior space of Pullman Town is revealing: *'We are born in a Pullman house, fed from the Pullman shops, taught in the Pullman school, catechised in the Pullman Church, and when we die we shall go to the Pullman Hell.'*

[51

It is only a small step from the company town of the nineteenth century to the present-day campuses of companies such as software manufacturer Microsoft or the electronics concern Samsung. The transition from life at the university to a working life has been reduced to a minimum at the Microsoft campus in the American town of Redmond. The surrounding greenery, the sports facilities, and the restaurants recall the university campus model. The Microsoft buildings are four storeys high at the most and have a cruciform structure. Just as on the student campus, you look out your office window on to grassy fields surrounded by pine trees. In the interior of the offices, the difference between working at Microsoft and studying has been made even smaller. School and work converge here. The offices look like student rooms and almost everyone works in leisure clothes.

OUTSIDERS AND INSIDERS

The Urban Container has been shaped along various lines. On the one hand, it developed from the company town model, whereas, on the other, the juxtaposition of a number of divergent social functions within spatial boundaries is an important characteristic. The latter ensures that proponents see a perfect reflection or reproduction of society in this structure. The world ceases to exist outside the Urban Container; the world unfolds within the Container. The company town described above helps us understand developments in countries such as Saudi Arabia and Jordan. There, the various features of the Urban Container are given shape in the *compound*. The compound is a living community for foreign employees of international enterprises who are doing local business. The rules within the fence of the compound are different from those outside. The social relationships are reversed. How should we regard this state of exception?

The strong Islamic rules in Saudi Arabia have an enormous impact on public life. Cinemas, theatres, discotheques and bars serving alcohol are all forbidden in Saudi society. Women may not drive cars or even cross the street with their faces uncovered. In the Western compounds, the codes of conduct are quite different. There are many places of entertainment and drinking alcohol is allowed. Women are allowed to drive and are not subject to obligatory dress codes. The city of Dhahran, in the east of Saudi Arabia, is one of the most sizeable compounds for foreigners and expatriates. The completely walled city is the headquarters of Aramco, the largest oil company in the world. Dhahran is home to around 11,300 people from the USA, Canada and the UK. The police, the hospital staff and the fire services are all under the auspices of the oil company and have their own rules and regulations. The central government of Saudi Arabia only gets involved in Dhahran life in emergencies.

The walls around the compound and the guarded entrance mark the transition to other rules and regulations in a very concrete manner. Within the periphery of the compound, people no longer adhere to the laws of the country but are subject to other guidelines or specific protocols. This regime of protocols is closely connected to the way of life and the culture of the community within the compound. What does the use of protocols mean? Protocols are not a new phenomenon. They have a long history in the army, in diplomacy and in health care, institutions that are deeply rooted in our society. Within these structures it is their task to realize the required conduct, based on a system of fixed agreements. We can define these as codes that prescribe a certain style of behaviour. Thus, protocols are not free of values or neutral. Just like technology, they are closely linked to social control. They produce their own normality because they demand of the people who stay in the delineated area of the Urban Container that they subject themselves to internal rules and that everyone displays the same behaviour.

At present, the number of protocols is rapidly increasing. Protocols prescribing the criteria that people's actions ought to satisfy are coming into force in the public space of cities. An excellent example is to be found in the public space of the Dutch city Rotterdam, where the so-called 'Rotterdam code' applies. This is a combination of various rules that the residents of the city must adhere to. This civil code demands that people speak Dutch on the streets, at school, at work, and at home. When the Urban Container permeates our society even further, protocols can be found everywhere. The typology of the Arabian compound is illustrative of this. In this compound, the rules of the Saudi Arabian law do not apply; there are detailed prescriptions that entail a unique normality or exceptional situation. Those protocols lead, as it were, to local jurisprudence. The exact aim of the control over the residents is not further defined, neither is the extent of its applicability. It is exercised by precisely-described internal rules that 'govern' life in the Container. In a reverse movement, the relationship [53 between architecture and life is closed. Refusing to accept a protocol means exclusion from the compound.

THE E-CITY: HAWAIIAN BEACHES, CLASSICAL PARKS, AND GREEK ARCHITECTURE

If we follow Michel Foucault, we agree that prison resembles the hospital, factory, and school. But why do the company town and the compound display so many similarities? The claim that a different society leads to a new space can also be reversed: a different space can result in a new society. Large-scale Urban Containers appear where information flows of the network society converge. This is the case at hubs or points of intersection of infrastructural networks. This is most visible in Asian cities such as Hong Kong, Shanghai and Beijing, where megastructures are being built at large infrastructural hubs such as metro and train stations.

In the early nineties, the local government of Hong Kong prescribed a strategy in which the *Housing Authority* was obliged to build 600,000 houses within fifteen years. In order to contain the strong population growth within the limited boundaries of its own territory, planners sought a housing model that was both flexible and efficient. The result is an apartment building that is called the 'harmony block'.

The first apartment blocks contained 16 to 18 apartments per floor and were built on a cruciform ground plan. The apartments are situated around a traffic core, independent of their orientation, in blocks of 38 storeys high. To compensate the lack of space – the average surface area per resident was around 11 m^2 in the first blocks – several towers were placed on a platform. As prosperity increases and the demand for larger apartments with more facilities grows, the project developers can adapt the harmony block to the requirements of the more prosperous Hong Kong resident. In this way, the Kingswood Villa project, with 15,880 apartments in 58 apartment blocks, was realized in the *Tin Shui Wai* Hong Kong city expansion. The neighbourhood offers the residents a 30-acre park in which a lake has been installed. A first-class hotel was taken as the standard for the facilities.

As a follow-on to Kingswood Villas, the harmony block is being used by an increasing number of Chinese project developers as the ideal model for luxury house-building projects. With advertising panels that cover complete walls, the developers attempt to entice new residents by evoking visions of Hawaiian beaches, classical parks, and Greek architecture. Buy the apartment and be part of an exclusive world without worries, is what the brochures sing out. Whereas communal facilities once served to compensate the lack of space in the high-rise blocks, the facilities are currently being deployed to realize a 'city within a city' that is relatively independent of its location and direct environment. Although the apartments in the luxury harmony block are not large in terms of surface area, the facilities in the platform under the high-rise blocks ensure that the residents never need to leave their model town. The chaos of urban traffic, the exhausting heat, crime, and noise pollution may reign outside. Inside, the residents have every conceivable amenity at their disposal, such as babysitters, servants, laundry service, newspaper and magazine delivery service, club houses, car parks, car maintenance, shuttlebus transport, etc.

In order to screen off the macro-interior of this added-value complex from the outside world, all the residents have a pass with a unique code. The prediction of a city in which people can only leave their flats, their street, and their neighbourhood with the help of an (individual) electronic chip pass has become reality.[28] Without private security services being necessary, undesirables can be rebuffed from the virtual Container. By making use of a smartcard linked to an electronic network, users can gain access to the various spaces in the Hong Kong harmony block. To which parts they can gain access depends on their membership, which can be extended as the residents wish. The e-network registers the way the residents live in order to be able to attune facilities and services to one another in an optimum fashion.

CONTROL FROM THE CRADLE TO THE GRAVE

Does the Urban Container function as a control laboratory? It is becoming increasingly obvious that the factor space is a fundamental dimension of our society. If we regard society from the standpoint of a control culture, which no longer operates on a basis of investigating crime but is oriented to excluding all possible risks instead, a last feature of the Container comes prominently into view. In the Container, the physical space is completely permeated by computer networks and monitoring techniques such as automatic detection and pattern-recognition cameras whose aim is to predict and prevent crime. Far in advance of the crime being committed, cameras identify individuals or groups as potential criminals on the basis of their behaviour. With an appeal to the protocols in force in the Container, the information is then used to remove these people or groups from the same delineated space, for preventative reasons.

[55

The boundaries of the nodal Containers are established by means of modern electronics, advanced computer programs, and interconnected databanks. Virtual moats protect the residents against an outside world they want nothing to do with: 'It's a dangerous world out there.' In this way, the physical Container moves increasingly to the background and makes way for a virtual space that can be actualized by means of smartcards and unique codes. With its emphasis on isolation and its combination of social functions, is the Urban Container the perfect architectonic expression of the pursuit of maximum security? Whatever the case, we can easily summarize the results of this culture of security, which is not only characterized by the application of new techniques such as video surveillance but also by harsher sanctions (*three strikes and you're out!*) and an expansion of the prison complex. Here, our anxiety proves itself. It seems as if something is constantly happening, but nothing is actually happening at all. With an acknowledgement to Guy Debord's *The Society of the Spectacle*, we can say: what appears is *safe*, what is *safe* appears.

CHAPTER 3

The Bankruptcy of the Street

DIscussions on the city are dominated by two discourses. The Urban Container is part of the first way of thinking. The previous chapter sketched its most important principles that are the basis of a revolutionary change in the notion of space. The first principle is that the institutions that had their own separate spaces in the disciplinary society are now participating in large-scale complexes where social functions such as shopping, living, work and education are united. This does not mean that the boundaries of these have been neutralized, they have merely been redivided. A first impulse toward a densification of space was visible in the company towns that were founded at the initiative of business sectors such as the mining, steel, car and wood industries in the nineteenth century. The second principle entails that a different regime of rules and sanctions applies within the Container than outside. Within the spatial boundaries of the compound, life is regulated by means of separate protocols. This means that reality within the Container differs from that outside the Container. The third principle covers the demarcation between inside and outside by means of digital networks or virtual city gates. The inner world of the Asian E-City is protected by the fact that every resident has been virtually codified. Virtual walls have replaced the physical construction of the Container.

These principles of the Urban Container fit seamlessly with the previous argument on the city with respect to the second discourse, the militarization of life. Since the early nineties, the government has been trying to reinforce its grasp on public space by deploying new monitoring technologies and codes of conduct in physical space. This fits into a development called *'Reclaim the Streets'*. In the UK and the USA, the government has begun to install detection and pattern recognition cameras on a large scale in public space. These not only have the aim of monitoring the behaviour of individuals in public space, but they are also used to 'steer' behaviour to a large extent. In London, the use of systems such as Closed Circuit Television (CCTV) has led to the Underground being equipped with a network consisting of thousands of cameras. In the public space of Chicago, an advanced system of cameras has been put into operation. It alerts the police when someone is wandering around apparently aimlessly on the streets, or is hanging around supposedly too long at a public building. Simply hanging around with your friends is definitely passé. The exclusion of security risks fits in with a strategy that David Garland refers to as 'responsibilization'. In this, security is a broad and shared liability that is not only the responsibility of the government. With slogans such as 'partnership', 'public-private co-operation', and 'active citizenship', this responsibility is further concretized.

[57

Which consequences do the development of the Urban Container and the militarization of life have for the public space of the city? What has ensured that squares, parks and streets have been public space or even the public domain until now? What is still public about these areas and how spatial is this publicness? Public space refers to the spatial-physical aspects of urban public life. By 'good' public space, we mean the result of the interaction between an urban space and the social or cultural use that residents and visitors make of it. This is called the 'public domain'. Although the public domain is also linked to works that are free of copyright, it primarily refers to a public area with a social function. It signifies a space in which we can share our opinions with others. According to the philosopher Hannah Arendt, this is the most important aspect of the relationships between citizens. In *The Human Condition* she states: *'The reality of the public realm relies on the simultaneous presence of innumerable perspectives and aspects in which the common world presents itself and for which no common measurement or denominator can ever be devised.'* [29] The exclusion of individuals or groups thus means that a halt is being called to the informal gathering of various social groups, cultures, lifestyles and ideas. In view of the importance that Hannah Arendt attaches to the public space with reference to the freedom of thinking, speech, opinion-forming and conviction of others, this space ought to be available to everyone in principle. But who currently occupies the public space of the *polis*?

THE WORLD OF HIKIKOMORI: 'MAM, WHERE IS MY FOOD?'

In Japanese cities, an increasing number of people are withdrawing from public space. Perhaps that is not so surprising in a country with 127 million inhabitants but it does not make the trend less spectacular. More than one million Japanese young people between twenty and thirty years old no longer leave their bedrooms. This phenomenon is referred to as *Hikikomori*, which means something like 'social retreat'. The young people have turned away from the streets, squares and markets in Tokyo, Kyoto and Osaka. To them, pubic space has become an empty space where nothing ever happens. They have shut themselves in their rooms and these 'screenagers' only maintain contact with the outside world via computers and internet connections.

Hikikomori is not a new phenomenon. It is a variant of a trend that arose as far back as the 1980s: *Otaku*. The Japanese word *otaku* has various meanings in everyday language. Originally it meant 'my house' but it is more frequently used as the personal pronoun 'you'. In Japanese, there are more than fifty different expressions for 'you'. Of all these variants, *otaku* is the polite way of addressing a person who is in an unclear social position in relation to yourself. Besides being a form of address, the word has also acquired another meaning. *Otaku* is also used as a collective name for teenagers – especially boys – who have a disproportionate interest in a single topic. Although their interest is primarily oriented toward typical Japanese phenomena such as anime, manga and video games, *Otaku* are also active in other areas: cars, music, uniforms, tools, etc. The fascination for these '*know-bots*' is translated into the collection of as much knowledge as possible in their field of interest. They are focused on all the information that can be found on their favourite theme. In a quest for the finest details, they attempt to outdo one another. They do not need to ride around in their favourite car all day or listen to their favourite music. They simply want to know everything about their favourite topic, right down to the most random details and then outshine the others by saying:

'Did you know that …?' and 'Oh, didn't you know that?'

Otaku are children of the media. To them, information is much more than a disposable article. Information is a fetish product. *Otaku* are always on the internet, looking for everything about their topic: *'With computers they get really involved. (…) They have a different rhythm, are awake for 40 hours and then sleep for 12.'* [30] As a result of the etymological meaning of *Otaku* as 'my house', the idea persisted that these were young people who never went out. In actual fact, this turns out not to be the case. *Otaku* function in a normal manner in society. There are quite a lot of *Otaku* among the student population, who encounter one another on various occasions such as trade fairs and events. Although many Japanese regard *Otaku* as freaks who are only interested in the latest flights of fashion, they term has not acquired negative connotation. For example, the electronics district of Akihabara is known as 'Otaku Town' among the residents of Tokyo. The science fiction writer William Gibson even refers to these young people kindly as 'passionate obsessives'. To him, an *Otaku* symbolizes the connoisseur in the information society. With one difference: their collected knowledge is no longer oriented toward concrete objects, but rather to data: *'Understanding Otaku-hood, I think, is one of the keys to understanding the culture of the web. There is something profoundly post-national about it, extra-geographic. We are all curators, in the post-modern world, whether we want to be or not.'* [31]

However, *Otaku* have quietly made way for the phenomenon called *Hikikomori*. An important cause of this change is the fact that internet has acquired a much wider application. Whereas internet was initially used as a medium to search for information, it is now linked to a virtual reality in which people communicate via chatboxes and are active by playing video games in groups or clans on online platforms. Despite the similarities, the way in which *Hikikomori* are treated in Japan is in stark contrast to what happens to *Otaku*. No positive connotation whatsoever is assigned to *Hikikomori*. Among Japanese young people, there is no one who is proud to be seen as *Hikikomori* or is proud to have this epithet. While *Otaku* mingle in everyday life, meet one another at markets and fairs, and are visibly present to others in the public space of the city, *Hikikomori* represent solitary retreat. Sometimes the young people do not come out of their rooms for five years. They spend their time playing computer games and surfing on the internet. Their parents place meals and drinks at the door to their room. The Japanese writer and film director Ryu Murakami calls them *'Japan's Lost Generation'*. In his view, they have reversed their lives: *'They sleep all day, wake up in the evening and stay up all night watching television or playing video games.'* [32]

Murakami relates the advent of *Hikikomori* to the enormous growth that the Japanese economy has made and the technological progress that has been made. In his opinion, the phenomenon is a form of stress and the consequence of the great demands that this society places on young people. It is not the first time that a certain period in our history has been connected to a syndrome. For instance, for a long time hysteria was regarded a typical illness of the nineteenth century. According to the erstwhile medical-psychiatric insights, biological factors were the cause of the fact that many women suffered from hysteria. Socio-political theories later ascribed the illness to the coercive role patterns between men and women. The deeply suppressed longing to assume a position equal to a man was expressed in attacks of hysteria that were regarded at the time as a protest of the woman against her impossible position. When women could participate fully in social traffic, with the advent of the right to vote and equal pay, this illness disappeared from society.

60]

Just as with hysteria, *Hikikomori* is also referred to as an illness. As a result of the large number of young people affected – 1.2 million – the Japanese Ministry of Health, Employment and Welfare even speaks of an epidemic. But Murakami emphasizes that it is a social phenomenon that is closely linked to the paradoxical situation in which present-day Japan finds itself: *'It is concerned with the increase of socially withdrawn kids, while at the same time it applauds gizmos like the new Sony PlayStation, which comes equipped with an Internet terminal and a DVD player. Technology like that has made it possible to produce animated movies and graphics, as well as conduct commercial transactions, without ever stepping out of the house. It inevitably fixes people in their individual space. In this information society, none of us can be free from being somewhat socially withdrawn.'* [33]

HOW PUBLIC SPACE IS BEING MOVED

Despite Murakami's provocative statement that Japan is being confronted by the perverse effects of a constant pursuit of technological

innovation, *Hikikomori* remain to many Japanese a nihilistic phenomenon in which the actions of the individual have become completely monomaniac. From the point of view of the Japanese, the *Hikikomori* youngsters are soulless creatures who have lost all contact with
our 'objective' reality. But viewed from the standpoint of the militarization of life and the advent of the Urban Container, as described in
the previous chapters, the phenomenon that an increasing number of
young people are withdrawing from the public space of the city and are
secluding themselves in a virtual space does raise a number of princi-
pled questions. These questions concentrate on the important theme
of resistance. Michel Foucault already observed that power cannot be
understood without resistance being assigned a place as well.[34] According to Foucault, power stirs up resistance. Without power relationships, there are no relationships of resistance. It is only when resistance can no longer be thought that there is nothing else beyond power. At that moment, power has been neutralized and ceases to exist. [61]

Speaking about resistance means that the public space must also
be taken into the argument. Expressions of resistance such as strikes,
disturbances, riots, or demonstrations have in common that they take
place in public life, in the physical environment of squares, buildings,
streets, bridges, and parks. *'If you want to change the city you have to
control the streets'*, is a well-known slogan of the *Reclaim the Streets*
cultural movement, which aims at reconquering the streets from
large-scale project developers and commercial companies and organizations. But if, in our theory-forming, we always allow the notion of
resistance to coincide with occurrences in public space, there is a risk
that resistance will be kidnapped by that same space. In other words,
what remains out of sight if we continue to interpret resistance as an
activity on the streets? Can the nihilistic and escapist phenomenon of
Hikikomori be seen as a form of resistance, for example?

The questions on resistance can be balanced against the power of
the American army, which extends into the virtual domain of war
games. Which forms of resistance are evoked by the presence of the
American army in virtual reality? Arabian video games give an elu-
cidating answer to this question. Everyone has witnessed how the
American army has committed itself to fighting terrorist forces on
various fronts worldwide. As a reaction to this, various Arabian countries have produced games in which a different perspective is shown
than in *America's Army*. In these games, the players learn to throw

stones at foreign soldiers, they shoot at Ariel Sharon, the former Israeli prime minister, and the blow themselves up amid a group of Israeli soldiers. In these games, the Americans are no longer the heroes and, more strikingly, the enemies are no longer Arabs.

JAMMING OR BLOCKING?

In the struggle for collective use of public space, two forms of resistance are remarkably conspicuous: *Culture Jamming* and *Reclaim the Streets*. The term *Culture Jamming*, which means both 'deregulating' and 'playing together spontaneously', was first used by the American band Negativland in 1984. With this, the group referred to playful activities such as the alteration of texts on billboards and the sabotage of other media expressions. By parodying advertisements and creatively processing billboards, the content of the commercial messages was radically changed. For example, in the Canadian magazine *Adbusters*, the word 'grease' was written over the smile of the hamburger clown Ronald McDonald. And in a parody on an advert for Nike sport shoes, the working situation in the Indonesian factories was outlined. This tactic of 'détournement' or reversal, which manipulates and mutilates the messages and significance of texts and images to create confusion in society, is related to those in all kinds of art movements in the avant-garde: from Dadaism and Surrealism, William Burroughs and Brion Gysin, to the situationism of Guy Debord.

Just like *Culture Jamming*, the cultural *Reclaim the Streets* movement (RTS) is oriented toward the physical space of the city. In the struggle to make unlimited and undisturbed use of public space, RTS installs 'Temporary Autonomous Zones' (TAZ). This term, borrowed from Hakim Bey, refers to the creation of free areas. In his work *The Temporary Autonomous Zone*, Bey draws the comparison with a guerrilla operation that suddenly looms up and vanishes again before the local authorities can get a grip on it. He speaks of *'microcosm of that "anarchist dream" of a free culture.'* [35] To the RTS, the TAZ is a perfect technique to locate the cracks in the current society and to occupy empty spaces, at least for a short time. The movement has its origins in London in the early 1990s. In 1994, it gained much publicity by an action against the construction of an urban circular, the M11, in the east of London. By squatting a disappropriated housing block and by blocking the streets, the demonstrators were successful in postponing the construction of the urban circular for several months. The action was embellished by a music sound system by means of which DJs and MCs treated those present to the latest dance music.

During the conference of the G8 in Birmingham on 16 May 1998, the mixture of politics and pleasure reached a climax. People across the entire world were mobilized by means of communication resources such as e-mail, websites, gsm and sms to support the ideas of the movement and to carry out actions against the privatization and increasing annexation of public space by multinationals. On that day in cities across the entire world, there were illegal street parties, some of which took place without incident while others ended as street battles. In the Netherlands, more than 800 dancing people blocked a motorway in Utrecht. In the Finnish city of Turku, 2000 people celebrated on one of the most important bridges in the city.[36]

[63

VIRTUALITY IS WHAT HITS BACK

What are the aims of these cultural movements? Is the resistance directed against the fragmentation of public space into separate microworlds of order and control, such as privately-managed interior spaces, large-scale covered shopping malls, and residential areas patrolled by security services? It is not without reason that the anti-globalist Naomi Klein states that the demand for a communal and free use of public space is an important objective of the present-day struggle in the city: 'As our communal spaces – town squares, streets, schools, farms, plants – are displaced by the ballooning marketplace, a spirit of resistance is taking hold around the world. People are reclaiming bits of nature and of culture, and saying "this is going to be public space".'[37] Whatever the aim of Culture Jamming and Reclaim the Streets may be, the street remains the favourite battleground where this struggle is fought out.[38] The same question repeatedly arises: How can we occupy the physical space of the polis?

The places where people can meet one another in freedom and exchange ideas have altered in the past few centuries. In the eighteenth century, coffee houses functioned as public meeting places where differences of opinion could be articulated and public opinion formed. In the nineteenth century, shopping alleys and publicly accessible libraries became the symbols of modern openness. Nowadays people speak of streets in the large department stores in cities such as Tokyo and New York. In those encapsulated boulevards, people promenade and groups of young people hang around the whole day long. Public space is not an autonomous area or undifferentiated unit; in other words: its identity is not a given fact. Besides the government, renowned multinationals have become an important factor when dealing with public space in the large cities and the determination of spatial policy. For example, the Walt Disney Company is not only engaged in amusement and theme parks, films and hotels. In 1991, Disney realized a residential neighbourhood called 'Celebration' in Orlando. This is regarded in America as being a leading example of New Urbanism. Celebration is the new world, but one according to Disney's rules and regulations. In Celebration, the values and norms from the previous century have been combined with the technology of tomorrow. In Celebration, the

nostalgic romanticism of front porches and rocking chairs goes hand in hand with modern technological facilities such as glass fibre cables and online communication. However, the influence of the Disney Company is not restricted to newly constructed housing estates in American cities. The influence of the Mickey Mouse empire is even more renowned for the cleansing and beautification of Times Square in New York. Partly at the insistence of Disney, who wished to build a theatre and entertainment complex in this district, the location was scourged of the typical phenomena of metropolitanism such as porno theatres, homeless people, and rundown premises.[39]

Because public space has many forms, we can ask ourselves whether or not this space is perhaps more than a physical location. For example, if *Hikikomori* is a manifestation of what the American author Howard Rheingold calls a 'virtual community', the question of the notion of resistance becomes even more salient. With the advent of a virtual reality, we are witnessing exceptional forms of resistance that manifest themselves beyond our 'objective' reality. Where are the cracks and empty spaces in our society where virtual resistance can nestle?[40]

THROWING PIXELS

Virtuality has become a fundamental element in the layout of our physical space. The physical structure is virtually occupied, as it were.

This has repressive consequences but also offers creative possibilities. The words 'virtual' and 'virtuality' have been borrowed from the Latin 'virtualis', which means 'non-existent' in classical Latin. Around 1700, 'virtual' and 'virtuality' were well-known terms in optics, particularly in the theory of the 'virtual image'. This referred to the objects we see in the mirror but do not actually exist. They are fictive representations that we perceive at the end of the reflected light rays that connect the object to the surface of the mirror and our eyes.[41] A century later, the concepts permeated mechanics in theories on virtual speed, virtual momentum, and virtual forces. There, the terms refer to the meaning the Greek philosopher Aristotle attached to the Greek idea of 'dynamis', which refers to a precisely determined possibility or potential that realizes itself as a solid form in the course of time. This potential cannot exist on its own. It is determined by the ultimate form and is thus not a substance in the true sense of the word. Its definitive appearance only exists because it has already been expressed in the 'materia'.

[65

In order to understand the various forms of resistance in the current global information economy, we must take virtuality in another significance. Manuel Castells calls the form of reality that arises and is processed by mediascapes of popular culture *'real virtuality'*.[42] With this concept, the Spanish sociologist rejects the idea that a virtual reality is separate from our physical reality. The reality of our culture is completely embedded in the media. The media have become so all-embracing that human experiences have been assigned a place there. As such, virtuality exercises an indelible and not-to-be-underestimated influence on our everyday activities. To understand the impact of this *real virtuality*, Arabian video games may offer a clarifying perspective.

The fact that games contain more than the expression 'it's only a game' might suggest is demonstrated by the role that games have been allocated in the conflict between Israel and Palestine, which has been dragging on for years. In the clash between the two peoples, the Palestinians use games as a means of resistance against the suppression and exploitation by Israel and the United States. The most well-known weapons in this struggle are the games *The Stone Throwers* (Hamza, 2000), *Under Ash* (Afkar Media, 2001), and *Special Force* (Hezbollah, 2003). Thus, the war not only takes place in the streets of Jerusalem, Tel Aviv or Hebron, but also in the virtual environment.

This expansion of the violent and armed struggle into the virtual world means that we must again study the meaning of resistance. Has resistance chosen the virtual environment as its platform of activity?

The fact that the muscle of the USA and other world powers extends into the virtual domain is not only shown by the fact that their armies use games as simulation devices and that the virtual and objective reality overlap in the experience of the soldiers. The presence of those countries in the virtual domain evokes a reaction and these active opposing forces form additional proof of the power of the USA and its allies. As an expression of America's worldwide war against terrorism, the Western game *Velvet-Strike* (Anne-Marie Schleiner, 2002) must certainly be mentioned. *Velvet-Strike* is directed in a peaceful way toward the violence that occurs between terrorists and military units in the well-known game of *Counterstrike* in which the armed conflict is fought out between teams of terrorists and SWATs.

66]

Velvet-Strike consists of a collection of images that can be sprayed like graffiti on the walls, ceilings and floors of the public space in the game *Counterstrike*. Captions and drawings can be downloaded from a website specially set up for that purpose and could be applied in a manner visible to the other players in the virtual environment of *Counterstrike* game. You could regard *Velvet-Strike* as a virtual 'détournement' or reversal because it breaks into *Counterstrike* space and makes unexpected and surprising comments on the actions of the players. In an interview, the maker of *Velvet-Strike*, Anne-Marie Schleiner, stated that this action not only elicits enthusiastic reactions but also strong protests from the players active on the *Counterstrike* servers: *'We received death threats and hate mails from every conceivable direction. I think a big part of the negative reaction to Velvet-Strike was anger over a woman becoming involved in what has become a very male culture. Another faction was 'patriotic' American boys who perceived our project as an affront on America. Our project was a series of anti-war protests and interventions. Of course others were positive or at least interested. And even the negative feedback I consider a success because it forced people to define their positions and also forced some strange people to come out of the woodwork (the sorts of people you see in Michael Moore's 'Bowling for Columbine').'* [43]

If we look at this virtual form of resistance from an Arab point of view, we see that *The Stone Throwers* was the first game to be deployed to influence the course of the struggle against Israel. The game

was created by the Syrian Mohamed Hamzeh and can be downloaded from a website with the name 'Damascus-Online'. To commemo-
rate the Palestinians who have died in the fights with the Israeli army,
the following message can be read on the internet site: *'To those who
lost their lives for the freedom of the homeland and all those who are
fighting for freedom – from Syria with love.'* Against a background of
the Al Aqsa Mosque in Jerusalem, the players take on armed Israeli soldiers. In contrast to Western games such as *Counterstrike, Full
Spectrum Warrior* and *America's Army*, they do not have an extensive arsenal of weapons. Stones are the only weapon they have at their
disposal. When the game is finished, the message appears that playing this game is not restricted to the virtual environment. The problem of *real virtuality* has more than one aspect. The players get to
hear that they have only killed Israeli soldiers in a virtual environment. Subsequently, a Palestinian funeral is shown, along with the
text *'This is the real world. Stop the killing of the innocents of Palestine before the game is really over'*. Isn't this a lesson in the continual movement from the real to the virtual world and back? The logic
of the movement rests on the fact that each virtuality eventually becomes reality and that each reality sinks into a virtual world, as the
Arab resistance against the dominance of Israel and the United States
demonstrates in *The Stone Throwers*.

[67

SUICIDE ATTACKS ARE EVERYWHERE

The importance of *The Stone Throwers* can hardly be overestimated.
Although the design and the interactive possibilities lag far behind
those in Western games, the game is extremely popular in the Arab
world. In the meantime, designers have come up with games that are
deployed as resistance against the Israeli occupation. A year after *The
Stone Throwers*, another game, *Under Ash*, was issued by the Syrian publisher Dar Al-Fikr. Twenty-one years after *Battlezone, Under
Ash* is the first Arab 3-D computer game. In this game, the player assumes the identity of a Palestinian boy with the name Ahmad, and
carries out a violent struggle against the Israelis. In every stage of the
game, the player is informed of the historical background to the Palestinian question. In the first part, Ahmad attempts to reach the Al
Aqsa Mosque in Jerusalem. If he reaches this alive, he must evacuate

his wounded Palestinian brothers, disarm Israeli soldiers, and repel military troops from the holy site. In another part of the game, Ahmad forces his way into a Jewish colony to raise the Palestinian flag. The last assignment takes place in the south of Lebanon, where he participates in a Lebanese guerrilla attack on an Israeli radar post. *Under Ash* has already had more than 500,000 downloads from the internet and more than 15,000 examples have been sold in the Middle East at $10 each.

The success of the games in the Arabian world led the Syrian publisher to issue another game with the title *Under Siege* (Afkar Media, 2004). It is the first game in which the main role has been allocated to a woman. The player can play a Palestinian woman who volunteers to be a suicide bomber in Israel. After having given her child to family members for safekeeping, she allows a hand grenade to explode in the midst of a division of Israeli soldiers. Just like *America's Army*, a

regime of strict rules and sanctions also applies in this game. Shooting innocent citizens leads to a deduction of points, with the remarkable detail that it does not matter whether these are Israeli of Palestinian citizens. The images in *Under Siege* show much resemblance to *Full Spectrum Warrior*, a game that was also developed by the American army. But whereas the conflict takes place in the capital of the fictive country of Zekistan in *Full Spectrum Warrior*, the action in *Under Siege* takes place between and on the roofs of the buildings in the occupied territories. *'We can't harvest peace unless we seed justice,'* explains Radwan Kasmiya, the manager of the game.

In *La volonté de savoir* (The Will to Knowledge), Michel Foucault states that in our relationship with power, there is not just one place of – as he articulates it – the *'Great Refusal: the soul of resistance, the focus of all rebellion, and the pure law of the revolutionary'*.[44] There are diverse forms of resistance, each of which has its own background. This is also indicated by the words of Mahmoud Rayya, a member of staff of the Hezbollah office that was responsible for the development of the game *Special Force*: *'Most games being offered on the market are games in which, unfortunately, the hero is an American, and he is coming to kill the terrorist, who is an Arab. We wanted to provide our youths with an alternative. Resistance is not confined to weapons. You also have to catch up with the ever-growing industries like the Internet and computer games.'*[45] The words of Rayya indicate that resistance repeatedly looms up at new places and in new forms. Games such as *The Stone Throwers* and *Under Ash* harmonize better with the experiential world of the young Palestinians than the traditional media like radio and newspapers. In the midst of daily violence, they comprise a different expression of the refusal to accept the existing situation of oppression and exploitation. The fact that the struggle now takes place in the virtual environment does not make the struggle less place-oriented. The conflicts are always directed to an exclusive power subject: Israel and the United States. In their struggle against the dominance of these countries, the Palestinian resistance has one concrete goal. In the games, the players are concerned with the liberation of the occupied territories and the foundation of an independent state of Palestine as a precondition of a definitive solution to the conflict. We call this coherence between resistance against a dominant power and the achievement of a concrete standpoint a 'liberation practice'.[46]

LIBERATION AND FREEDOM PRACTICES

Liberation practices are not the same as freedom practices. There is a qualitative difference between these. In a liberation practice, the conflict is against the dominance of another country. In classical terms, the resistance is oriented toward the law or the rules of another state. In a freedom practice, the experience is more extensive. A new identity begins to take shape and a positive self-experience arises. Which forms do the positive effects of this pursuit of freedom assume? And in which ways does a new self-awareness come to the fore? Besides the resistance to the oppression and exploitation by Israel and the United States, the games *The Stone Throwers*, *Under Ash* and *Under Siege* have in common that they evince a communal Arabian identity. In the virtual environment of these games, the participating players experience their identity in a specific manner. According to the creators, the *Under Siege* game should therefore not be regarded as a response to the American war game *America's Army*. Radwan Kasmiya believes that *Under Siege* offers a new form of identity: '*This is not a game about killing (...) We are telling a story. It's not about desperation, it's about sacrificing your life to let others live.*' The way in which players in Western war games are disciplined and normalized are the subject of discussion in this game. In this way, Arabian players experience an alternative to the dominant picture in which every soldier who is fighting for the good cause always comes from the American army. In an interview, the project director of the game *Under Ash*, Hassan Salem, claims that a different argument is created in Arab games: *'We're trying to counterbalance the poisonous ideas conveyed by American video games to our children. Our primary aim is educational: We want the new generation, which doesn't listen to the news, to learn about the Palestinian cause.'* [47]

The success of these war games, which are used by very diverse groups to ensure their voices are heard, also evokes tension and problems. Video games are not value-free or neutral media. This fact has not escaped the Israeli government. To the question concerning how Israel regards the game *Special Force*, the spokesperson of the Ministry of Foreign Affairs, Ron Prosor, replied: *'We don't see them as games but as part of an educational process which is preventing any chance of real peace.'* [48] In terms of realism, there is thus little difference between the game *Special Force*, issued by the central Internet office of Hezbollah, and the American games on terrorism. It must be remarked that the Arab games are permeated by an anti-Israel iconography. *'Fight, resist, destroy your enemy in the game of force and victory,'* is the slogan of *Special Force*.

With the assistance of maps, video pictures, and other archive material, the computer section of Hezbollah has created virtual versions of conflict situations that actually took place in reality. In addition, the game includes a separate training programme in which players learn to shoot at Israeli and military figures such as the former Prime Minister Ariel Sharon. Just as in other Arabian games, a player in *Special Force* operates from the perspective of a young Palestinian who participates in the jihad. He arrives in the same situation as the members of Hezbollah and finds himself, just like them, on enemy ground opposite the Israeli troops. According to Bilal Zain, one of the creators, the game serves as a counterweight against the propaganda of Western games. *'We want others to know our land is occupied, our people are imprisoned in Israeli jails, our houses are being demolished,'* he says.[49]

The argument of a freedom practice focuses on a different question than that in a liberation practice. The question not only involves 'What are we fighting against?' but also: 'Who are we?'. This question ought to be seen in the light of Foucault's comments on the article *'Was ist Aufklärung?'* (What is Enlightenment?, 1784) by the German philosopher Immanuel Kant. The question that is the cen-

70]

tral theme of this text is also the question about the present day. What is happening today? Foucault translates Kant's question as 'What are we in our actuality?'. With this, he wishes to breach the universal and objective nature of 'Who are we?'.[50] Besides the struggle against the power of a state, the virtual space of games also accommodates the fight for one's own identity and self-image. Apart from referring to oneself, a distinct character with its own vocabulary also arises. A specific form of community or subjectivity arises in the relationship to oneself, the other players, and the involvement in the game.[51] In that respect, games are truth games by means of which the Palestinians can constitute their own history and identity. On this basis, we can assign a positive value to this freedom practice. A new subjectivity is produced in the form of a coherent identity. In the virtual reality of games, the Arabs have positioned themselves in a different manner in the power game of political relations: they present themselves not as terrorists but as freedom fighters. With this, games turn out not only to cover a view of the enemy and the introduction of new rules and sanctions, but also the forming of a social identity and community.

[71

SONIC
URBANITY

PART TWO

CHAPTER 1

The Audio-Hallucinatory
Spheres of the City

AS the world becomes smaller and we can travel increasingly easily and cheaply, many city administrations attach high priority to putting their own city on the map. Cities compete with one another to obtain more residents and more tourists, and also to accommodate the headquarters of multinationals such as Shell, Siemens or Sony. The quality of the architectural structure and the representative character of the city form essential preconditions for this, just as cultural facilities also play a major role in this rivalry. A branch of the Guggenheim Museum is welcomed by every metropolis as a godsend. One only has to think of Bilbao in this context. The construction of the subsidiary of the Guggenheim Museum, designed by Frank Gehry, transformed this once-modest fishing village into a part of a global network of people, services, and information. In China, cities such as Beijing and Shanghai flaunt themselves by inviting internationally renowned architects to generate a new building repertoire. 'Old' cities such as Berlin, London and Paris, join this trend and give their centres a new impulse with new architectonic icons. The image is the city's best advocate. The suggestion is evoked that the most important qualities of the city are its situation and the beauty of its buildings. This so-called 'postcard architecture', by means of which cities try to distinguish themselves from one another, places the emphasis on the permanent or durable character of a city and harmonizes with the ideas of the nineteenth-century urban planners who believed that the soul or identity of a city rested in the run of the streets, the allure of the buildings, and the size of the squares.

However, you might wonder whether the discussion on the city ought not to be seen in a wider framework. After all, a city is more than a skyscraper, a museum or a library. There is also another, less tangible form of urbanity. This urbanity is directed toward forms of co-habitation. In order to understand better the scope of the city, we should ask ourselves how this immaterial urbanity arises. We should devote attention to the related issues of the relationship between interior and exterior, between who belongs here and who doesn't. The ideas of Peter Sloterdijk offer various starting points. In his work entitled *Sphären*, this German philosopher describes how, from prehistoric times onward, groups have demarcated their territory by emitting sounds. Due to the fact that people dwell in bells of sounds, they can distinguish between the group of which they are a part and their direct surroundings. Sloterdijk refers to these environments as 'spheres'. While the various hordes lived separately from one another in the prehistoric days, we are now connected to one another worldwide via a network of roads, aviation and shipping routes, internet, satellites, and cables. With the advent of these logistic and digital networks, mutual distances have become smaller. Despite the overwhelming scale and fineness of these networks, we ought not to forget, however, that sound still plays an important role in the creation of specific living environments. For a lengthy period, sound did not play a role in the representation of the city. However, if we do allow scope for it when considering the city, our concept of urbanity will also change.

THE DISCONNECTION OF ARCHIGRAM

The architecture of the British Archigram is a first indication that urbanity is more than the materialized embedding of modernity. Archigram – a combination of the words 'architecture' and 'telegram' – is the name of the magazine in which David Greene, Warren Chalk, Peter Cook, Mike Webb, Ron Herron, and Dennis Crompton express their dissatisfaction with the limited horizon of current architectural practice. Until the end of the sixties, the Archigram architects did not operate as a closely-knit team; they worked relatively independently of one another in various architectural offices and educational institutions. Thanks to the efforts of the English architectural critic Reyner Banham, the group became known under the name of their magazine, Archigram. They wrote manifesto-like texts for this magazine and called for an end to the dominance of the functional architecture deployed to rebuild Britain after the Second World War. In their view, this architecture did not keep pace with the upcoming information society. In a passionate plea for the potential of technological developments and popular mass culture, they claimed that architecture has to accept the challenge of uniting technology and popular culture. This fusion ought to lead to people being able to free themselves from the restrictive bonds with their direct living environment. Architecture ought to be committed to the struggle against the static and durable character of the built environment. In Archigram's view, the new information era is now dictated by movement, as embodied in space capsules, robots, and computers.

[77

In the early sixties, influenced by the designs of Richard Buckminster Fuller, Archigram designed a series of sphere-shaped capsules.[1] These are equipped with all the necessary facilities, and enable the residents to form a sealed and close community. An excellent example is the *Living Pod* design, which is shaped like a moon capsule. The skin of this capsule contains all the facilities of a normal house. The exceptional feature of this accommodation is that it is mobile. Detached from its direct environment, the *Living Pod* can be installed anywhere in the world. The *Capsules* design presents series of capsules linked to a high vertical concrete core. At the top there is a crane that can link up a new sphere at any given moment. In another design entitled *Blow-out Village*, the capsules are attached to a fan-like structure of telescopic arms so that they can float at various heights above the landscape. The arms are equipped with a large transparent dome that can be drawn across the area. With these spherical and mobile designs, the Archigram members created sealed interior worlds that could function autonomously and independently of their direct surroundings. The sphere inhabitant could regulate everything himself.

'*The pre-packaged frozen lunch is more important than Palladio,*' claimed Peter Cook in 1967, convinced that the most important innovations take place in domains outside architecture: in space travel, the packaging world, communications media, and the car industry. For this reason the group believes that architectural practice must be extended to other aspects of cultural production, to the exuberant pop culture and pioneering technologies of space travel. The scope of architecture must be pushed beyond strict, bureaucratic boundaries and elitist aesthetics. It must dissolve in everyday life, that is Archigram's deepest wish, for only in this way can life itself become architecture. To give the residents of modern cities more freedom of movement in an environment that they can shape themselves, Archigram abandons ideas of durability and identity, aspects which are particularly characteristic of postcard architecture. To them, hot-air balloons, landscapes, and space capsules are also architectonic items. In Archigram's *Moving City*, the city as a whole has been put into a mobile capsule. In the way they move through the landscape on extendable legs, the capsules resemble fat insects made of steel. They berth like cruise ships at old static cities such as New York, London and Amsterdam. In the Egyptian desert, they make the ancient pyramids look like miniature toys.

78]

Because the layout of physical space is becoming increasingly less important to Archigram, the members of the group no longer limit their designs to spheres. Under the influence of sweeping developments in the field of information and communication, their radical proposals are becoming less and less material. *Tuned Suburb* is equipped with satellite dishes and space-travel technology. With this, Archigram demonstrates that residents of suburban neighbourhoods can have the same intense experiences as those in the centre of a large metropolis. Themes such as invisibility, weightlessness, transience, and mobility are becoming the focus of their attention. Architecture is being disconnected from the domain of the city and is issuing into projects such as *Quietly Technologised Folk Suburbias, Crater City* and *Hedgerow Village* which are subtle links between popular media and activities organized on the spot.

Although Buckminster Fuller wanted to build a geodesic dome over the area of 22nd Street to 64th Street in Manhattan in 1962, in order to protect the residents against air pollution, for example, Archigram no longer needs the material sphere. With underground buildings, weightless balloons, and new communications technologies, the group creates spherical interior spaces or *Plug-in Cities* that are held together by invisible threads and tunnels. The spheres acquire an urban character when the residents have logged in. This type of development reached a climax in 1969 when Archigram won an architectural competition for the design of an entertainment centre on a piece of reclaimed land on the coast of Monaco. The plan consisted of an underground dome with a park above it. The roof, covered with trees and grass, has service openings in a grid of six metres by six. Visitors can plug in their parasol, telephone, and television here. Making use of the facilities of the underlying building, sunbathers can watch television in the park and discuss the latest news by telephone with friends. To make the disconnection of modern humankind complete, the design provides an underground hall that is large enough to accommodate ice-hockey games, circus performances, and rock concerts.[2] Unfortunately, the project faltered during the excavation of the site due to problems with ground water. Due to a lack of political support, the project was not continued. Despite the fact that it was never implemented, the project did draw attention to the increasing influence of information and communications technologies upon present-day culture and on the layout of urban space in particular.

[79

DETROIT: THE NEEDLE AND THE CITY

Should we assume, just like Archigram, that the city no longer needs an own location? In the vision of this group of architects, the city is no longer fixed at one place, as postcard architecture would like to have us believe. The Archigram projects demonstrate that the city has become movable. This means that the substantiation of urban space can at least be uncoupled from its concrete, physical manifestation. In order to define this non-materialized form of space more precisely, we shall go one step further and leave the Archigram designs, which rely on dynamics and mobility, behind us. Instead, we shall direct our attention to expressions of the pop culture which has grown to become a worldwide phenomenon under the influence of the globalization process.

The history of dance music is closely linked to the city. Ten years before *pirate radios* such as Kool FM, Pulse and Defection sent jungle music into London's ether and Paul Elstak and Speedy J surprised Rotterdam with the accelerated gabber beats, techno music arrived in Detroit in the eighties. Techno connects the industrial sounds of the white German musicians Kraftwerk with the artificial disco from New York and the futurism in the black music of artists such as Sun Ra, Herbie Hancock, Miles Davis, and Funkadelic. The most renowned producers include the duo Juan Atkins and Rick Davis, who operate under the name Cybotron – a combination of 'cybo(rg)' and '(elec)tron(ics)'. In 1984, they gave Detroit the name under which the city is still known: *'Tech-noh Cit-ehh'* exclaims the distorted voice of Rick Davis in the number of the same name. The number covers the situation in which the city found itself at the end of the seventies, after the race riots, the departure of the car industry, the large-scale population movements, and the construction of highways through densely populated areas. The disappearance of the most important industry, which changed the city into an archipelago of enclaves, expansive asphalt areas, and abandoned factory yards – in short, the demise of Detroit – did not induce in Atkins and Davis nostalgic deliberations on the illustrious past of their place of residence. *'You can look at* 80] *the state of Detroit as a plus. We're at the forefront here. When the new technology came in, Detroit collapsed as an industrial city, but Detroit is Techno City: it's getting better, it's coming back around,'* claims Atkins, full of confidence.

In their music, musicians such as Cybotron, Model 500, Derrick May, and Kevin Saunderson do not go looking for the soul or identity of Detroit. Due to the many aliases that Kevin Saunderson uses to sell his music – The Bad Boys, E-Dancer, Esray, K.S. Experience, Inter-City, Inner City, Kaos, Keynotes, Master Reese, and Tronikhouse – Detroit seems larger than it actually is. According to Derrick May, the music is no longer concerned with the name of the artist or the deepest feelings of the musicians, but rather everything depends on a distinct flavour. He says: *'It's the emptiness in the city that puts the wholeness in the music. It's like a blind person can smell and touch and can sense things that a person with eyes would never notice. And I tend to think a lot of us here in Detroit have been blind: blinded by what was happening around us. And we sort of took those other senses and enhanced them, and that's how the music developed.'* Detroit techno connects a certain impression to unarticulated ideas. The distinct flavour arises by linking sounds to the typical features of the city. The sounds of techno create a new collective and auditive shell for Detroit. They generate a spherical space in which the listener can form a mental picture of a city without having to visit it in real life. Driving along a quiet highway through a desolate neighbourhood, as articulated in the number *Cosmic Cars* by Cybotron in 1982, is nothing less than an urban sensation: '*Stepping on the gas. Stepping on the gas in my cosmic car.*'

PUT YOUR HANDS UP 4 DETROIT, IT'S A LOVELY CITY

The sounds referred to by the Canadian composer Murray Schafer as 'soundscape' or 'sonosphere' draw the lovers of techno into the interior of a psycho-acoustic living environment. The rhythm of the music not only stimulates dancers to make robot-like, spastic movements, the music also evokes an immediate and topical sensation of the city of Detroit. A sort of space is generated here that is other than the one that actually appears before us. For a long time, people regarded physical space as an objective stage or absolute unit. Space was regarded as a linear and independent fact, an objective stage on which objects had their own place and social processes occurred.[3] In this vision, the perceiver and the object are opposite one another, and there is a neutral space between them.[4] In an acoustic or sonic space, one is always at the centre. The ear has no opposite and has no frontal view of an object that is at a distance. In the context of the techno, urban space must therefore be approached differently. Urban spatiality, in the meaning of permanently 'hearing one another' and 'seeing one another', is also evoked by means of sounds from pop music.

[81

Besides the city being independent of its location (as the designs of Archigram demonstrated), we can now conclude that the city is bounded by time. Because a city can be actualized in the mediascapes of pop music at any given moment, it no longer has fixed co-ordinates or points. Our urban environment is only a history of spheres or shared spatial constellations. From a similar perspective, the situationist Gilles Ivain sketched in his article *Formulary For a New Urbanism*, which dates as far back as 1953, a city with districts that covers the entire range of human feelings and emotions: the bizarre neighbourhood, the happy neighbourhood, the noble and tragic neighbourhood, the historical neighbourhood, the useful neighbourhood, the sinister neighbourhood, and the death neighbourhood. In this gathering of spheres, the sinister neighbourhood is the equivalent of the districts with a bad reputation where unsavoury characters hang around in creepy bars.

The history of the genesis of techno gives us insight into the way in which this electronic dance music manages to actualize an urban spatiality worldwide. The term 'techno' is first used in *The Third Wave*, a book by the American futurologist Alvin Toffler. Applying the term 'techno-sphere' he describes the changes that have taken place down through the ages. Toffler claims that large-scale changes have taken place three times in the history of mankind. The first was the agricultural revolution that required more than a thousand years to reach maturity. Then followed the industrial revolution, with the upsurge of factories, standardization, specialization, and mass production. During this process of change, which lasted around three hundred years, there arose a distinction between the producer and the consumer. In our time, this process of industrialization has been inundated under a wave of digitization. After the agricultural revolution and the industrial revolution, the digital revolution, with its information and communications technologies, is the third fundamental change in human history. Toffler introduced the concept 'techno-sphere' to describe the

system in which energy use, production methods, and distribution are joined, whereas, in his view, 'techno-rebels' are the most important people in our information age: *'nuclear engineers, bio-chemists, physicians, public health officials, and geneticists as well as millions of ordinary citizens.'* [5]

Inspired by Toffler's ideas, Atkins and Davies interpreted the first video games as forms of expression of urban spatialities in the digital era. In their view, the spatial infrastructure of video games offers new opportunities to meet one another in a different way. They refer to the framework that ensures an open system of connections as the 'Game Grid': *'We used a lot of video terms to refer to real-life situations. We conceived of the streets or the environment as being like the Game Grid. And Cybotron was considered a 'super-sprite'. Certain images in a video programme are referred to as 'sprites', and a super-sprite had certain powers on the game-grid that a regular sprite didn't have.'* [6] The multiple spatial dimensions of video games inspire them to create numbers such as *Alleys Of Your Mind, Cosmic Cars*, and *Clear*. But it is in the number called *Techno City* that a coherent and inspired urban spatiality is realized with sound as the most important representational and connecting element.

Techno City is Atkins and Davies' answer to the film *Metropolis* by Fritz Lang. *Metropolis* was shot in the UFA (Universum Film Aktiengesellschaft) Neu Babelsberg studios near Berlin in 1925 and 1926, and had its première on 10 January 1927. The film deals with the

inequality of employers and employees, but owes its renown largely to the vertiginous décor in which the story takes place. Congested
trunk roads function as a bridge between skyscrapers, and aeroplanes
make breath-taking dives through this mesh of roads. To Davies,
Metropolis is the ultimate proof that a city subject to the laws of natural physics can also be evoked by the fleeting and unstable nature of
a soundscape: *"Techno City' was the electronic village. It was divided into different sectors. I'd watched Fritz Lang's 'Metropolis' – which
had the privileged sector in the clouds and the underground worker's
city. I thought there should be three sectors: the idea was that a person
could be born and raised in Techno City – the worker's city – but what
he wanted to do was work his way to the cybodrome where artists and
intellectuals reside. There would be no Moloch, but all sorts of diver-
sions, games, electronic instruments. Techno City was the equivalent
of the ghetto in Detroit: on Woodward Avenue the pimps, pushers etc.
get overlooked by the Renaissance Tower.'*   [83

'YOUR PLACE OR MINE?'

The ability of pop music to generate its own new environment leads
us to deliberate on the various spatialities of the city. If we can create
an immune system by means of sound, where are we in the city? In
other words, how are these inner worlds related to the outside world
of the city?

In his comprehensive study *Sphären*, Peter Sloterdijk rejects the
idea that space is a stand-alone entity that is detached from objects
and subjects. In his view, the production of sound is the oldest and
most efficient way of creating a space. The *Sphären* project therefore
covers the history of mankind and the place that humans have occupied in the world down through the years. To Sloterdijk, the traditional question in philosophy is no longer: 'What is mankind?' but rather 'Where is mankind?'. In his response to the question, he compares
people living together in small groups in prehistoric times with cast-
aways who are drifting on wooden rafts on the open sea. Prehistoric humans roamed around in relative isolation in the wild. Although
they lived in a certain harmony with the natural environment, they
needed sounds to demarcate their territory. By murmuring, singing, talking, and clapping, the members of the group imposed a dis-

tinction between the group and the surrounding environment. The size of the inner world was thus determined by the range of the voice. Each group had its own timbre and unique pitch. These specific properties allowed sound to function as a point of recognition and as a connecting link between the various members of the group. The sounds brought about a communal continuum.

Sloterdijk observed that, to prehistoric humans, living in small nomadic communities and surrounded by overwhelming nature, a good sphere was a survival sphere. The original meaning of 'sphere' derived from the Greek *sphaira*, is 'ball'. In a more general meaning, a sphere is a ball-shaped experiential space between two or more people who have a close mutual relationship. In a natural environment full of danger, sound spheres offer the group members protection and safe accommodation. But which significance do these shared spatial constellations have in the discussion on the present-day urban space? To which new, world-embracing spatialities are the spheres of popular culture leading?

Sloterdijk's antipathy to pop music prevents him from establishing the relationship between the social aspects of human society and pop culture. He has an extremely negative appraisal of the popular media culture's offensive. In his opinion, pop music, as heard all over the world, contributes to the dismantling of the sonosphere of the global society.[7] Sloterdijk claims that the assault that this music makes on the ears of the world population is unique in its sort. In unmistakable terms, Sloterdijk gathers all music into one heap and concludes that Western amusement music, after a period of exchange with music styles from the East and South, has developed into a vulgar music hybrid that has conquered the entire world. In his view, the uniformity of pop music is proof that a regression is taking place, making the ears of the world population insensitive to everything that is new.[8] The same musical dictates are issuing from loudspeakers over the entire world, the same tonising effects, and the same standardized and tonal phrases.[9] In short, pop music has reached the stage that it produces identical rhythmical and harmonic formulas in every corner of the world.

There is little doubt that the homogenizing power of the popular media is enormous. The sounds around us are no longer produced by humans alone or by wild nature. New media such as the radio, television, internet, MP3 players and iPods have replaced clapping, singing and murmuring as a means of communication, and ensure that pop

84]

music is ubiquitously present. However, the fact that the same musical dictates repeatedly recur does not have such a disastrous effect as Sloterdijk maintains. The repetition of tonal phrases, effects and formulas is one of the essential properties of pop music. In addition, a different context for a quote or a sample automatically leads to new interpretations. More important than the judgement on quality is the fact that music constructs a coherent social space among the listeners. This 'psycho-acoustic' space is characterized by a double movement. It arises as a result of the members of the group, while it brings people together at the same time. The sound ensures that the group manifests itself as a unit, while the individual members feel that they have become a part of the group.

URBAN: A NEW SPATIALITY?

An ever-recurring question is: What is the relationship between a being together and the physical co-ordinates of the city? From this standpoint, you can ask what Archigram and Detroit techno see as a problem. How to save the city? How to be saved from the city? Whatever the case, the similarities between them are striking. They share a fascination for the city that has been prised loose from its concrete boundaries. They are not alone in this. To an ever increasing degree, a range of products and activities, varying from music styles, clothes, perfumes and jewellery to sneakers are being regarded as being typically urban. It is not easy to explain how substantial the sphere of influence of the city actually is. Baggy denim jeans with conspicuous zips, buttons, and sewn-on pockets are called 'urban jeans'. Urban Lingerie is the trend that combines ultra-feminine underwear with the coarse style of hip-hop clothes. The sunglasses from the Adidas Kill Loop series mix trends from sports clothes with the raw energy of the city. In the shops, they are on sale as Urban Sunglasses, in much the same way as gold and diamond-studded watches, belts and chains are sold as typically Urban. In the hip-hop culture, the term 'Urban Car' represents a four-wheel driven jeep or SUV, preferably an Escalade model Cadillac. Urban Entertainment is being made for Afro-Americans under the theme 'life in the big city'. Urban Skating, Urban Golf, Urban Climbing, Urban Freeflow, Urban Base Jumping, Urban Streetraces, and Urban Soccer are the names of the latest sports.

And Urban Arts is the overarching name for art forms that range from graffiti, stickers and posters to various forms of street dancing.

Despite the fact that all these products and activities are distant from the city as such, they evoke strong associations with urbanity. And that brings us to the core issue. How should we regard the identity of the city when the city is so tangibly present in this arsenal of dispersed products and activities? In the answer to this question, we anticipate the idea that the city is both placeless and time-bounded in our media-based society. We propose that a unique space has arisen in the popular Urban youth culture, with its own history and own logic, and which can serve as the background for the debate on the process of urbanization.

Various writers have argued that people sell the Urban culture short when they see it as synonymous with immigrant culture. Despite the fact that this postulation of equivalence between immigrant ('black') and Urban does not do justice to their diversity, there has been increasing appropriation of 'urban culture' by the hip-hop and post-hip-hop culture since the mid-nineties.[10] Although the collective term 'Urban' originates from the Latin word *urbanus* meaning 'city' or 'civilized', the term is generally used to refer to the world of hip-hop and R&B.[11] In hip-hop and R&B, this adjective is linked to minorities who know how to survive in the poorest neighbourhoods of the metropolis. The street is the source of all wisdom and the place where authenticity, trust and credibility are not yet empty phrases. The street not only stands for 'real', it also brings up the necessary credits if you belong to this environment. *'I'm still Jenny from the block (...) I know where I came from (from the Bronx)'* sings Jennifer Lopez in the number *Jenny From the Block* in 2002. The Latino-American star borrows her identity from the archetype of gangsters (*gangstas*), pimps, whores (*bitches*), and other residents (*playas*) of the cities in the USA.

At first sight, societal developments bounded by place and time seem to be represented by the Urban youth culture. Nevertheless, the history of this urban empire has acquired a wider context by means of a sophisticated product and marketing mechanism. The way in which this merchandising can lead to a shared spatiality can be reconstructed on the basis of the story of the Simmons family. The well-educated Russell Simmons grew up in the Hollis neighbourhood of Queens in New York in the sixties. At the time it was a mixed neighbourhood for the middle class. His younger brother Joseph, who would later become famous as Reverend Run of the rap group Run-DMC, described the neighbourhood as *'nice homes, manicured gardens and everything.'* [12] During his study at City College, Russell Simmons organized various hip-hop parties, but he gained national fame when he founded the Def Jam record label with Rick Rubin in 1984. Simmons did not restrict himself to issuing the music of LL Cool J, Beastie Boys, Public Enemy and EPMD, he also embarked on a new adventure six years later with his company Rush Communications, which is now an important motor behind the present-day Urban culture.

Rush Communications is made up of various subsidiary enterprises. In addition to the production of live shows, television programmes, magazines, and energy drinks, the company also produces sports clothes that are brought on to the market with 'street credibility' under the label Phat Fashion. Phat Fashion presents itself with the prestige of the Ivy League, the universities and colleges in North-east [87 America that are highly regarded and have an excellent reputation in the field of education. The company describes its clothing line as *'a mixture of the hip-hop culture of the streets and the preppy culture of the Ivy League'*. Phat Fashion consists of the sections Phat Farm, Baby Phat, and Phat Farm Kids. Whereas Phat Farm is a men's line, Baby Phat, under the management of Simmons ex-wife, the former Chanel model Kimora Lee Simmons, is oriented to young prosperous women. Phat Farm has now been sold to the clothing giant Kellwood Co. for 140 million dollars. The diversity of the company is indicated by the fact that Rush Communications also has at its disposal an ideal network that organizes congresses throughout America with the aims of making the black population more politically aware and of increasing the percentage of voters among them. Furthermore, with the Rush Card, the company is attempting to reach the forty-five million Americans who do not have their own bank account or credit. With these pre-paid cards, these people are less dependent on money offices for depositing of money. While every transaction costs one dollar, the card can be purchased for 20 dollars.

The term 'urban' gained more profile when Russell Simmons's brother, Joseph 'Run' Simmons, launched the rap group Run-DMC along with Darryl 'DMC' McDaniel and Jam Master Jay. Having grown up in the Hollis suburb and not in the rundown slums of New York, the members of the Run DMC emphatically distance themselves from their respectable background. Rick Rubin, the co-founder of Def Jam, articulated their disparity with the street as follows: *'With Run-DMC and the suburban rap school we looked at ghetto life as a cowboy movie. To us, it was like Clint Eastwood. We could talk about those things because they weren't that close to home.'* [13] The outfit typical of Run DMC – black clothes with white Adidas trainers – only arose after a performance in the Bronx. Ridiculed by the public because of their clothes and origins in the 'soft' neighbourhood of Queens, the group spent the first money they earned with record sales on the latest fashion from Jamaica Road. In 1986, they made their breakthrough with the number *Walk This Way* and with their characteristic clothing.

It can hardly be denied that entertainment concerns such as Rush Communications, which link the underside of life in the metropolis to products and activities such as clothes, shoes, prepaid cards, and congresses, are making their mark on urban life. The closeness of the street and commercial success is shown by the Death Row record label of Suge Knight and Dr. Dre from Los Angeles, which is associated to the Bloods street gang. During a performance on the well-known American television programme *Saturday Night Live*, the biggest star of Death Row, the rapper Snoop 'Doggy' Dogg, wore a Tommy Hilfiger shirt. This television show has been broadcast for more than thirty years, can be received in the United States via more than 219 different transmitters, and each show is watched by an average of 8.2 million viewers. Until Snoop Dogg's performance, the market profile of Hilfiger was similar to that of Calvin Klein; the clothes of Hilfiger were mainly worn by white middle-aged men from mid-America. After Snoop Dogg's television appearance in 1994, the sales figures for the brand rose by 90 million dollars. Tommy Hilfiger subsequently designed more baggy clothes as a response to the demand for 'street-wear' from the big cities on the west and east coast of the United States.

THE INTERMEDIAL SPACE OF AN URBAN EMPIRE

Just like Detroit techno, Urban youth culture also has the ability to bring together individuals and to colour the experience of urbanity. With Detroit, we have seen that information and communications technologies keep inner spaces together and create a new form of urbanity. Those same forms of worldwide communication enable cross-fertilization between nightclubs, radio broadcasts, record labels, and tracks such as *Techno City* and *Cosmic Cars*. Also, they enable that a coherent and shared urban spatiality can be generated at any given moment. How does this experience of urbanity take shape in Urban culture? What do the products and activities that are covered by the most attractive adjective in youth culture have in common?

In the video clip *Drop It Like It's Hot* (2004) by the rappers Snoop 'Doggy' Dogg and Pharrell Williams, the city radiates in size and grandeur. 'Snooop Dooog, clic-clac-clic-clac, Snooop Dooog' goes the beat, produced by the clicking sounds of the tongues of the two superstars. The sonic minimalism of the number returns in the pictures of the video clip directed by Paul Hunter. The two rappers are standing in a black-and-white décor. The place of action alternates with their favourite urban icons: a black Rolls Royce, a low-rider three-wheeler, a belt studded with jewels, mobile phones, and Ice Cream gym shoes. Without the city being explicitly on show, the black-and-white images evoke a specific urban experience and spatiality in which the rappers play the main role. [89

How can we explain this form of detached urbanity? The conclusion does not seem too difficult to draw. The video clip of Snoop Dogg and Pharrell Williams demonstrates that the rapid urbanization of our living environment is not restricted to the physical space of the large cities where the majority of the world population will live over thirty years, if we believe the figures of the United Nations. This process of urbanization is also taking shape via other spaces and processes.

The seductive Urban sound world makes the city conceivable and tangible via another means. The sounds and rhythms are connected to a symbolic world. Clothes, cars, and jewels becoming 'charged' objects because they actualize what the city represents. And in doing so, Urban creates a different urban space between its public and the various products and activities. Although Urban only relies on its roots to a certain extent, it demonstrates that the city cannot only be regarded as a collection of 'artefacts' that take their genesis and significance from a specific historical context. Although the Italian architect Aldo Rossi argued in his book *The Architecture of the City* that *'through architecture perhaps more than any other point of view one can arrive at a comprehensive vision of the city and an understanding of its struc-*

ture', Urban indicates that another analysis of the city is possible.[14] Rossi's idea that the design knowledge for the future lies in the existing buildings that have proved themselves down through the years is thus much too one-sided.

The foundation of a city is not a once-off event. That would mean that everything would be fixed forever. However, the city assumes a recognizable form outside the concrete layout of its physical space. Pop culture shows that the various media processes create space for a personal experiential world. This experiential world is not embedded in the physical environment but is the dynamic result of an urban experience that is evoked by divergent products and activities. Between the sunglasses, cars, lingerie, jewels, and clothes of the stars who are clad in their most chic ghetto clothes, an urban experience is woven. It is not without reason that Hype Williams, the director of Urban video clips, observes: *'Whatever continent you're on, the cool kids have the urban look.'* The inspired urban space that nineteenth-century urban planners dreamed of is now evoked in the context of Urban youth culture in a manner involving interrelated media. In this, the contours of the city are no longer drawn along geographical lines nor is its appearance determined by the distribution of wealth and power. Here the diversity of media in popular culture determines the urbanity, in which the city dissolves in an audio-visual sphere of significance that is constantly actualized by the same expressions of these media.

WHAT HAVE YOU BUILT TODAY?

People are sphere builders. In stating this, have we arrived at the point that urbanity no longer requires geographical determination or defining architecture? It is becoming increasingly clear that the city is thus expanding and that, in the course of time, it will be all-embracing. It seems to be moving in all directions, like an autonomous force. The corresponding process of urbanization must not only be regarded geographically, regardless of how impressive the physical expansion of the city actually is. There are also other processes that are part of this urbanization. The intermedial urban spatiality that Urban culture creates by linking the city to a miscellaneous collection of products and activities is a striking example of this. This type of development must be taken into account in any deliberation on the ongoing changes in the process of urbanization. Which new spatiality is created as a result of this? What is different about it? In short, we can state that, in order to understand fully the process of urbanization, it is necessary to examine the various spatialities in close conjunction. Now that the city has expanded beyond physical matter into the mediascapes of popular culture, we should at least regard urbanity in relation to the effects of processes other than physical ones.

CHAPTER 2

Sampladelic Spatialities

IN the feature film *Dancer in the Dark* (2000) by the Danish director Lars von Trier, the Icelandic singer Björk plays the role of the musical-lover Selma Jeskova. She lives with her ten-year-old son in a trailer somewhere in the United States. A congenital eye sickness is making her gradually blind. Her son has the same illness but an eye operation could prevent him undergoing the same tragic fate as his mother. In order to pay for the expensive operation, Selma works long hours in the local metal factory. We witness how Selma's condition gradually worsens. But although she sees less and less, her world does not become darker. The picture never becomes black. The less she sees, the more she loses herself in the colourful world of her daydreams, where she plays the leading role in her own musical. The sounds from her surroundings are transformed into cheerful rhythms and melodies. Even when she loses her job, has killed her neighbour, and is ultimately brought to justice, her naive and optimistic core still remains. The intense perception of sounds offers her an escape to a different, positive world of sounds and spheres.

In *Dancer in the Dark*, Von Trier makes it clear that sound can generate an environment bound by time but detached from the place one occupies. When we relate this to present-day pop culture, we see that films, games and music surround the earth with their alternative environments. They create shared spatialities, even for people that are far away from one another. The question arises as to which conceptual techniques are applied to evoke these spatialities. In which ways do we have control of the design of the intermedial space in popular styles such as techno, hip-hop and R&B? When we restrict ourselves to this music, we see that semi-acoustic environments or soundscapes with their own spatial effects can be designed by means of new techniques such as montage and sampling. These techniques are the foundation of subtly designed spaces that are akin to Von Trier's acoustic alternative for Selma's visual reality. Because these soundscapes can be reproduced, the concept of 'community' has acquired different substantiation. Montage and sampling are techniques that detach us from our social and physical environment. The spatialities constructed by montage and sampling offer an environment for social relationships between people who are in the grasp of the pop media. Accordingly, sampling is a perfect, present-day technique to generate the spherical spatiality of the sound bell. While the communal sound bell was aimed at giving our prehistoric forefathers a safe and protected environment so that they could survive, and thus had an evolutionary element, the semi-acoustic world of the twenty-first century has a different goal. Electronic globalization, which is partly created by the mediascapes of pop culture, has initiated a massive population migration toward a new, synthetic world.

[93

By means of the Afrofuturism people's movement, we wish to demonstrate that screening off from exterior influences, which Peter Sloterdijk admirably describes in his *Sphären* trilogy, also occurs in a sonic world whose residents are widely disseminated. Without allowing ourselves to be dragged along by new developments, or dismissing new technologies as instruments of pure illusion, we believe that sampling can elucidate how communities that are rooted in expressions of popular culture can be formed by means of sonic techniques. The German pop philosopher Diederich Diederichsen once said that in present-day dance music a sound stands for an entire community.[15] The last word on this statement has not been uttered, not even after Von Trier's film. After all, it is not yet clear along which sonic escape routes active humans will detach themselves from the primacy of their physical environments.

HOW SOUND ACQUIRES A SPATIAL DIMENSION

The first opportunity to reproduce sound arose halfway through the nineteenth century. Until then, making music or listening to it was a unique event that was related to place and time. To listen to a piece of music, one had to go to the market square, the bar, or the concert hall. As soon as the musicians stopped playing, the sounds vanished forever. It was impossible to listen to music again under the same circumstances. In addition, it was not possible to be certain whether or not the piece of music played was identical to the previous performance. There was no means of checking this, apart from looking at the sheet music. This elusive quality of music expired when Wilhelm Weber attached a pig's hair to one of the prongs of his tuning fork in 1830. For the first time, sound became tangible. It was expressed in the curve frequency of the tuning fork. By allowing the hair to vibrate on a glass covered in soot, the various pitches and sounds thus became visible to the eye.

Elaborating on this idea, the Parisian printer Édouard-Léon Scott de Martinville fixed a needle to a membrane in 1857. As soon as the membrane began to resonate, the needle also began to vibrate with a movement that left its traces on a rotating glass cylinder that was covered with a black pigment. Scott de Martinville thus managed to visualize sound by means of his 'phonautograph'. The sound machine was applied almost immediately in research on languages and dialects. In an attempt to reach some kind of standardization or homogenization of the various national languages, academics used Scott de Martinville's phonautograph to determine the standard for the ideal pronunciation.[16]

Ten years later, the inventor Thomas Edison, who suffered from poor hearing, came up with the idea of combining the working of the phonautograph with that of the Willis brand of typewriter. With this phonograph or 'speaking machine' it was possible to record sound and play it back. 'Hello?' was the first word that Edison recorded with his pioneering device. Shortly after Edison's invention, the German-American electro-technician Emile Berliner thought up the flat version of the cylindrical sound carrier of the phonograph. He replaced the phonograph roll with a disc with spiral-shaped grooves so that the sound waves were no longer recorded vertically but horizontally. Although the disc could not record sound, the discs had the great advantage that they were much cheaper in production and distribution.

The development that began at the beginning of the century led to the extraordinary situation that, at the end of the century, sound could be reproduced without much loss of quality. For the first time, it was possible to repeat musical pieces and sounds. Once the musical pieces had been recorded on a sound carrier, they could be experienced as three-dimension spaces. The consequence of being able to reproduce sound was that it was extracted from a strict time dimension. The techniques by means of which sound could be recorded drew it into another dimension, a spatial dimension.[17] Having become increasingly familiar with the details, a listener could meander around in the sound recording and lose himself in it. We can state that recorded sound has architectonic qualities, it offers 'accommodation' and an 'entrance' to the listener. Just as a space surrounded by walls and floors, this space also has a demarcation between inside and out. The sound recording allows us to experience the space that is recorded on a specific sound carrier. For example, recordings of shrieking monkeys, fluttering birds, and rustling leaves evoke the spatial experience of the jungle. But the sonic space also has another quality. Hearing sounds also means 'belonging to' those sounds. From this perspective, sound creates a specific social space that is a symbol for a community, as we shall later see. This ensures that the listener enters into a continuum of sounds. As we previously saw with the techno from Detroit, these sound techniques prise the listener loose from his or her direct physical 'sounding board' and welcome him or her in a specific sonic spatiality.

[95

This process of prising loose has been comprehensively studied by the French musician Pierre Schaeffer, who was educated as a sound engineer at the École Polytechnique in Paris. From 1942 onward, Schaeffer performed research at *Radiodiffusion Télévision Française* (RTF) on musical acoustics in electronic music. The Parisian media company furnished Schaeffer with all possible resources: phonographic turntables, sound recording equipment, facilities to cut recording tapes, mixers, and access to the library of the RTF in which all kinds of sounds and sound effects are stored. To Schaeffer, listening to sound of which the source was not directly visible or recognizable was an exceptional perception. In the sixth century BC, this way of listening had been practised by the students of the Greek philosopher Pythagoras.[18] They listened to the lessons of their teacher for five years while he taught them from behind a curtain. Following Pythagoras, Schaeffer called this manner of perceiving sound 'listening acousmatically'. This literally means hearing a sound without seeing the source that produces it. Schaeffer was not interested in the source of the sound or the instrument, he devoted his endeavour to what people hear in the sound that comes out the loudspeakers. Later the Canadian composer Murray Schafer would refer to these sounds as 'schizophony': sounds without a source. The sounds no longer refer to a recognizable environment or a natural event that has occurred previously.

DIRECTING SOUND

As one of the first sound engineers, Pierre Schaeffer discovered that a stand-alone sound environment can be assembled by means of a sound tape. By comparing music with the genre of the film and with theatre, he was convinced that the new technologies offered unsuspected possibilities for making music: *'Photography, whether the fact be denied or admitted, has completely upset music ... for all that, tra-*
ditional music is not denied; any more than theater is supplanted by the cinema. Something new has been added, a new art of sound. Am I wrong in calling it music?' [19] After the breakthrough of the gramophone disc, Schaeffer exchanged sheet music for the sound studio. Locking himself in his sound laboratory, *Club d'Essai,* Schaeffer researched the possibilities of the studio and he recorded compositions that were compiled from different sound recordings.

By chance, Schaeffer discovered new rhythms that were caused by the gramophone needle getting stuck on the record. He then understood that changes in the playing speed and the direction in which the disc was played could be regarded as instrumental properties of the record. Schaeffer became fascinated by the possibility of isolating sound and then further mixing it in his musical pieces. With the tape recorder, the call from Italian futurists to allow the noise of the metropolis to be a part of musical pieces could be honoured. Under the influence of the Italian composer Luigi Russolo, Schaeffer refers to the pieces that he compiles from sounds from his environment as *musique concrète.* With this term, he wishes to emphasize the difference with the *musique abstraite* that arises via the 'detour' of musical notation and a conductor. As a fully-fledged DJ, Schaeffer created his first composition *Concert de Bruits* in 1948, by changing the speed and direction of play of gramophone records, and by making loops of certain grooves on the record during a live performance. His next composition *Etude aux Chemins de Fer* (1948) is a montage of sounds that he recorded with a tape recorder in a train station in Paris. In that same year, Schaeffer broadcasts on national radio a composition that consists completely of recordings of train whistles, pots and pans, boats, percussion instruments, and piano sounds.

In fact, the possibilities of new sound techniques are best described in the renowned essay entitled *The Work of Art in the Age of Mechanical Reproduction* (1936) by the German thinker Walter Benjamin. Although Benjamin does not refer to the reproduction of sound in this work, he observed in general that the mechanical reproduction of an original artwork has drastic consequences for art. *'For the first time in world history, mechanical reproduction emancipates the work of art from its parasitical dependence on ritual. (...) From a photographic negative, for example, one can make any number of prints; to ask for the "authentic" print makes no sense,'* writes Benjamin.[20] In this essay, he compares modern film to traditional painting. The cameraman resembles the surgeon, the painter resembles the magician. The surgeon cuts into the body of the patient, the magician heals the patient by placing his hand on his body. Benjamin extends the comparison when he states that the cameraman penetrates reality whereas the painter maintains a natural distance to reality. By assembling various fragments, the cameraman constructs a new version of the same reality: *'It manages to assure us of an immense and unexpected field of action.'* The montage technique offers the opportunity to perceive a different world. Close-ups, slow motion and strange camera perspectives lead to new experiences that did not exist prior to the advent of film.

[97

The montage techniques that Benjamin describes in *The Work of Art in the Age of Mechanical Reproduction* can be applied to music with the aid of the sound tape. Because the sound quality of the magnetic tape could not be compared to that of a gramophone record in the period before the Second World War, it took longer for this montage technique to be applied in the medium of sound than it did in the medium of film. It was only halfway through the twentieth century that changes began to occur in this realm, partly due to the work of Pierre Schaeffer. The tape recorder turned out to be the most suitable medium for making sound recordings that could later be reproduced. Whereas the gramophone record is primarily useful for making copies of an original recording, the tape recorder is more suitable for the production of those originals because the technology is simpler and cheaper. Just as with film, the sound tape can be cut and sound fragments can be assembled in a different order of sequence. In this context, Pierre Schaeffer speaks of a 'sonic object', a stand-alone specific sonic spatiality with its own details and effects.

A MIGRATION TO THE FUTURE

How does sound manage to escape from our direct environment? Or, to put it more precisely, how does the advent of new sound techniques influence the way in which listeners are related to one another? After the first discoveries of Pierre Schaeffer, avant-gardist composers such as Karlheinz Stockhausen and Edgard Varèse experimented in *Club d'Essai* with the application of electronic techniques in their work. However, only when the techniques of the sound tape penetrate the sensory space of pop music is there truly mention of world-embracing spheres with an unprecedented social power. To quote Gilles Deleuze, sound can '*invoke a new people*'. For example, various black artists used various sonic techniques to construct an alternative world for their own community from the end of the fifties onward. Seeking a better world, sound is closely linked to an 'away from here' attitude with a concrete escape route.

In his article *Black to the Future: Afro-futurism 1.0*, the theorist Mark Dery demonstrated that this does not involve an individual flight but rather a broad social movement in which science fiction and futuristic themes play an important role. He refers to this movement as 'Afrofuturism'.[21] Kodwo Eshun explains it as a connective sonic fiction in which stories, concepts, and ideas are communicated by means of sound and are only partly visualized by means of images. In this speculative musical fiction, Afro-American themes are treated in the context of present-day techno culture.[22] On the basis of the work of black musicians and producers, Dery concluded that black Americans live in a permanent state of alienation. In his view, they are descended from hostages who were kidnapped from their place of birth by extra-terrestrial creatures. They live in a science fiction nightmare in which their movements are needlessly frustrated by invisible and impenetrable force fields of intolerance.

Afrofuturism shows us a different representation of the future than the one we know from the well-known examples from film and literature, where the metaphors from Fritz Lang's *Metropolis* (1927),

98]

the illustrations of Frank R. Paul for Hugo Gernsback's fanzine *Amazing Stories* (1926-1929), and Disneyland's *Tomorrowland* are the leading models. These sketch the future primarily in images, but, as Afrofuturism demonstrates, sound is also a component of the escape route. Jimi Hendrix's *Electric Ladyland* (1968), Miles Davis's *On the Corner* (1972), Herbie Hancock's *Headhunters* (1973), and *The Adventures of Grandmaster Flash on the Wheels of Steel* (1981) by Grandmaster Flash and The Furious Five have convinced Mark Dery of the existence of a different kind of futurism, a future veiled in rhythms and sounds. One of the first Afronauts was the free-jazz musician Sun Ra (1914-1993). Although his passport states that he was born as Herman 'Sunny' Blount in the American city of Birmingham, Sun Ra really came from Saturn and arrived on Earth to play inspired music from the universe in conjunction with his band Arkestra. The titles of his records, such as *The Heliocentric Worlds of Sun Ra, Vol. I* from 1965, and numbers such as *The Cosmos* and *Of Heavenly Things* form the proof of life beyond the planet Earth. The appearance of Sun Ra himself, his texts and the sounds of his free jazz refer to life in an infinite multiverse.

[99

Sun Ra is not the only one who arrived on Earth. The Jamaican dub-producer Scratch Lee Perry also vehemently denies that he was born on Earth: *'I am an alien from the other world, from outer space, I don't have no land, no estate, no property, no house. Not on this earth. I live in space – I'm only a visitor here.'* In the sixties and seventies, Perry was part of an extensive scene of Jamaican producers and musicians who continually tried to surpass one another with new rhythms, texts and vocal styles to make more people enthusiastic about the local dance clubs. During a production for the artist Duke Reid, Perry's colleague King Tubby discovered that he could use the tape recorder to detach a voice from the background sounds. This montage technique soon reached the Black Ark studio of Scratch Lee Perry. Using various techniques and effects, Perry supplied definitive proof of his extraterrestrial origins. With drop-out, equalization, delays, speed-ups, spatial echoes, reverb, flange, phase, noise gates, echo feedbacks, shotgun snare drums, and rubber bass, he mixed the indefinable sounds of his universe.[23] In this way, he produced in the studio sounds that we shall never hear in the world around us. With their montage techniques, these black artists are at the basis of a shared sonic spatiality that forms the link between fellow-travellers who have swarmed out across the entire world: across the northern part of South America, the Caribbean, the east of Central America, the United States, Canada, the United Kingdom, and Africa. This induces the author Paul Gilroy to compare in his book *The Black Atlantic: Modernity and Double Consciousness* the dissemination of the 'kidnapped' Africans to the diaspora of the Jewish people.

Which role does music play in the design of life? In other words, how can music become political? The British sociologist Stuart Hall deals with the significance of music for the identity of the black communities around the Atlantic Ocean. Music plays an important role in this transatlantic community in the creation of a social dynamics and identity.[24] Traditionally, black people have occupied a marginal position in the culture of the countries where they were introduced as slaves. For a long time, music was one of the few forms in which they could express themselves and exchange stories, information, and ideas on their African origins and the diaspora of the black community. The extra-terrestrial domain that Afrofuturism is seeking is the last stage in this process. The significance of sounds and rhythms reaches further than mere sound: music as a non-physical meeting place.

SAMPLING SONIC SPACE

With the introduction of the Mirage DSK-1 digital sampler in the mid-eighties, the montage techniques used by Grandmaster Flash, Scratch Lee Perry and King Tubby came within reach of every music lover. This digital montage machine, produced by Ensoniq, is a complete boxed sound studio that can be operated by means of a few buttons and controls. The Mirage DSK-1 is an 8-bit, 32 KHz computer that can write, read, store, scan, record and play sound. The device converts the recorded sounds into binary data and they can be repeatedly played at every desired speed and in any desired context without loss of quality. In scientific terms, sampling is defined as the procedure that gathers exactly as much data from a certain continuum as is needed to effectively simulate this continuum while using as little as possible storage space. The number of samples per time unit is known as the 'sample rate'.

When we look at the applications, we see that the sampler has primarily been used as a quoting machine right from the outset. The sampler is mainly popular because existing music fragments can be recorded and then replayed on a keyboard in any desired tempo. In this way, effects comparable to the scratches and cuts that are created in hip-hop by means of gramophones and records are also possible here, with the difference that the analogous system requires much greater skill. Every record has to be meticulously examined for sounds and grooves. Using a cross-fader on the mixer, the DJ can suggest a continuum between two records. The first sampler-users mastered the play of disappropriation, re-appropriation and appropriation down to the finest details. Disappropriation, or sonic theft, occurs when artists borrow sound fragments for their own numbers. In this way, sampling opens a new discussion on counterfeit and copying, the role of the author, quotes and quoting. In a sample, the distinction between original and copy, artist and connoisseur almost disappears.

The deployment of the sampler indicates that the technique of sampling is a variant on the montage technique of the tape recorder. [101 More than fifty years before the sampler was discovered, the tape recorder made use of the same technique. Sampling improves montage, or rather, the sampler improves the tape recorder. The functions of the tape recorder are embodied in the sampler. In principle, the *copy & paste* command on the computer is also a montage technique. The sampler has not only assumed the montage technique from the tape recorder, the associated sound concepts have also been taken over by the sampler. The construction of a new environment and the corresponding deconstruction, the dis-, re- and appropriation of existing material are all actions that can be performed by the sampler.

Nonetheless, the sampler is more than a digital tape recorder. Whereas extremely expensive recording studios were needed for montage technique, a sampler is an instrument that almost everyone can afford. Moreover, it is easy to operate. The complicated and labour-intensive montage techniques that Pierre Schaeffer used for his *musique concrète* have become superfluous with the advent of the sampler. The magnetic tapes no longer need to be cut, taped together, and recorded again. It is possible to allow real-time fragments to flow into one another and to distort them. The fact that sound has become digital is at least as important as the easy operation of the sampler and its accessibility to a large group of people. As a result, sound fragments can now be mutually combined in such a way that it is no longer possible to hear that they involve two different elements. Fragments can be seamlessly linked to one another up to an increase or decrease in speed of twenty per cent.

With the sampler, we enter the digital era, a period in which Pierre Schaeffer's acousmatic listening becomes a new event. There is a genuine explosion of music styles that take the sampler as their basic instrument. The English pop theorist Simon Reynolds refers to these music styles as 'sampladelia'. Styles such as trip-hop, techno, jungle, drum & bass, clickhouse, post-rock, jazzdance, and UK-garage are all known under this collective term. In sampladelia, cutting sound fragments is the basis of the mutation of source material into new sounds that seem to issue from imaginary or inconceivable instruments.[25] Accordingly, Reynolds uses 'sampladelia' as a term to describe the revolutionary consequences of the distorted music that is made using the sampler and other forms of digital technology: *'Its a radical break with the ideals of real-time interactive playing and natural acoustic space that still govern most music-making.'*[26]

102]

'THIS TOWN'S A DIFFERENT TOWN TODAY' (AM)

Anyone who thinks up a new rhythm also discovers a new way of experiencing the world.[27] The English theorist and founder of the Hyperdub label, Steve Goodman, sees a relationship in the number of sampled beats per minute and the forming of communities. He speaks of *speedtribes*, communities that are held together and distinguish themselves from others by a shared enthusiasm for the speed of their favourite music. The members of the *speedtribes* encounter one another in musical environments with their own specific beat rates. For example, reggae and dub have 0 to 80 beats per minute (bpm). The beat rate of hip-hop, trip-hop, dancehall and R&B ranges from 80 to 120 bpm. Most sampladelia have between 120 and 145 bpm. House, techno, and breakbeat-oriented music have a speed of 120 to 130 bpm. The fastest music styles include jungle, drum & bass, and gabber. While jungle and drum & bass vary between 145 and 180 bpm, gabber even reaches 220 bpm. Young people who share the same ideas on clothes, dancing, language, and drugs use gather around the beat rates of these various music styles.

Which concrete properties are characteristic of the communities that arise on the basis of the sounds and rhythms of the sampladelic spatialities? Features such as religion, race, gender or origins are certainly not a binding factor. As such, these communities do not conform to the classical notions of *Gemeinschaft*, as the German sociologist Ferdinand Tönnies defined it in his book *Gemeinschaft und Gesellschaft*, published in 1887. In Tönnies' theoretical model, each community is a mixture between *Gemeinschaft* and *Gesellschaft*. In a *Gemeinschaft*, individuals are oriented toward the group and toward themselves. They are guided by communal values and convictions. The *Gemeinschaft* is characterized by strong personal relationships and family bonds and relatively simple social institutions. The family is the ideal example of a *Gemeinschaft*. In Tönnies' view, the upsurge of modernity has meant the gradual replacement of the *Gemeinschaft* by the *Gesellschaft*. After Tönnies, sociology has remained unsure about how a *Gemeinschaft* can survive in modern society.

With the electronic globalization of the Earth by iPods, internet, radio and television, the notion of the community must be sought in a different direction. Every link with the nineteenth-century idea of *Gemeinschaft* has vanished. The sociologist Craig Calhoun speaks of the secularization of the concept of community. He argues: '*Community life can be understood as the life people live in dense, multiplex, relatively autonomous networks of social relationship. Community life, thus, is not a place or simply a small-scale population aggregate, but a mode of relating, variable in extent.*'[28] Following on from this, we wish to refer to the social relationships that arise as a consequence of sounds and rhythms as 'sound communities'. The coherence, unity, and the survival of the group – major notions for every form of community – are not based on physical proximity but rather on shared sounds and rhythms. The power and seduction of sound are strong enough to bring people together without there being mention of a transcending morality or overarching identity as the guiding principle. In this case, they are restless and asymmetrical groups that can be defined as spatial and process multiples.[29]

[103

THE SEDUCTION OF A SAMPLADELIC SPATIALITY

Two striking developments were linked to the advent of technical reproduction facilities for sound. First of all, techniques such as montage and sampling enabled people to assign spatial qualities to sound.

When we listen to music, we hear a different space than the one in which we are physically situated. Furthermore, these spatialities are not abstract and neutral environments. Specific stories, symbols and knowledge are shared in these environments. In order to answer the question of how rhythm and sound unify people in a community, we must understand the relationship between the spatial and the social aspects of sound.

In his novel *Mumbo Jumbo* (1972), Ishmael Reed writes about the link between the spatial and the social domains by referring to a magical piece of text entitled *Jes Grew*. Jes Grew is a term that Reed learned from the American human rights activist and theorist James Weldon Johnson (1871-1938). Johnson used the expression to describe the advent of ragtime music. Jes Grew is a bastardization of *just grew*. Making use of this, Jes Grew in *Mumbo Jumbo* stands for *'African diasporic cultures that live and evolve in the forms of gesture, music, dance, visual culture, epistemology, and language, crossing geography and generations by moving from carrier tot carrier and thus threatening the knowledge monopoly of the "West"'.* [30] Reed describes the diaspora of the black community as the spreading of a virus. Viruses differ from bacteria and other forms of life in that they cannot reproduce on their own. They cannot survive autonomously. Viruses survive by attaching themselves to a living cell of another organism and 'injecting' hereditary material into it. The sound virus infects individuals and brings them together in sound communities. Listeners become carriers and sources of infection due to the fact that the virus jumps from carrier to carrier.

Invisible to the human eye, the virus also stimulates an acute reaction in the bodies of each individual. The way this infection works is shown by the effect of various sound waves on our bodies. Each part of the human body has its own frequency. The higher frequencies of audible sound set the fingers in motion, while the lower frequencies activate the energy centre in the body just under the stomach. In the frequencies that are inaudible to humans, under 20 Hz and above 2 KHz, other parts of the body react with vibrations. Around 17 Hz, the eyeballs begin to vibrate in such a way that visual hallucinations occur. [31]

These physical reactions alone show that it is almost impossible to remain neutral or distant within the sampled environment of popular music. Sonic spaces are spaces in which concepts such as 'distance' or 'opposite' become redundant. Surrounded by a sound bell of 360 degrees, the listener is always in the middle of a sonic spatiality. This centre is not a static place. Pulses, tones, ticks, fuzz, melodies and beats are the periphery that embraces the listener. Everything moves and everything resounds due to the simultaneity of the various sounds. After all, don't sounds penetrate walls in order to abduct us? One could say that sound opens all doors. In a negative connotation, noisy neighbours and sound pollution demonstrate this daily. The acoustic space of a sonic spatiality or force field has soft boundaries rather than hard ones. It is a constant process of genesis or intensification in which only extremes seem to be valid. It appeals to us directly, as an affect. It will continue to seduce us and move us through any material whatsoever.

THE URBAN EFFECT OF GRIME

The most recent musical seduction from London – Grime – combines many of the above-mentioned sonic-spatiality qualities. Grime arose as a dark version of UK-garage that had little success outside London, but was known for the excessive parties where people drank cocktails and champagne while dressed in expensive designer clothes. Grime is a part of the British hard-core continuum. This continuum is based on the ultra-rapid breakbeat dance music that arose in the eighties and spread out in music styles such as acid house, bleep & bass, breakbeat house, Belgian hardcore, jungle, Rotterdam gabber, big beat, and speed garage. The continuum of this sample-oriented music mutates continually. The vibe of the music moves with developments in other realms, such as those of fashion and drugs.

Grime can be divided into two styles. In the one style, everything revolves around the *Master of Ceremony* or the *MC*. The striking feature of the MC style, which is represented by artists such as Dizzee Rascal, Wiley, and Roll Deep Crew, is the strong London accent and the speed of the raps. Whereas the MC was subordinate to the DJ in earlier mutations of the hardcore continuum, the MC has now acquired the main role in Grime. In contrast to hip-hop, where samples from old soul and funk records serve as the background, the Grime MC raps to the slowed-down breakbeat of rave music, thus breaching its trance technique. If a sense of trance threatens to arise among the listeners, it is rudely banished by fragments of texts about the harsh world of London underprivileged neighbourhoods. Grime seems to have chosen this schizophrenia as its basic attitude and finds it subversion and *raison d'être* there. '*What do you call it?/ Garage?/ What do you call it?/ Urban?/ 2-Step?/ Tell us what you call it?*', asks Wiley desperately in the number '*Wot Do U Call It?*'.

The other Grime movement, called 'sublow' and 'dubstep' focuses on the specific rhythms and basses of the music style. Sound samples from texts from gangster and sci-fi films, the sawtooth sounds of video games such as *Donkey Kong* (Arcade, 1981) and *Super Mario* (Arcade, 1983), the sounds of pistol shots and the simple ringtones of mobile phones create a unique field of tension. Both computer games and pistols are symbolic of the tension and leisure activities in East London, where violence and gunfights are becoming increasingly common. According to Grime star Dizzee – '*I wear my trousers ridiculously low*' – Rascal, it is no more than normal to carry weapons such as a Mac10: '*People want to make an impression, it's fashion, it just their culture.*' The urbanscape of Grime is thus no literal interpretation of urban sounds, as Pierre Schaeffer pursued in his *musique concrète*. Grime is a collection of city sounds of popular media. In conjunction, they evoke a new experience. Grime makes it clear that the sounds from cliché games or ringtones are every bit as much as part of the city as the cries of seagulls or the hum of cars and the subway. In Grime, the inhabited world has landed in a media particle accelerator in which physical constellations such as cities are influenced by signs, sounds, and people.

106]

ARCHITECTURE OF THE SKY

Sound is pure intensity. Nothing evokes quite such an intense, collective experience as sound does. According to Gilles Deleuze and Félix Guattari, this is also its greatest threat, or – to use their words – this is the source of the fascist threat of sound. Much more than the visual violence of flags and banners, drums and trumpets lead people and armies in a race to the ravine: '*Colors do not move people. Flags can do nothing without trumpets.*' [32] Nevertheless, this does not mean that the developments instigated by the reproducibility of sound will lead to an all-embracing environment. The worlds in the sonic domain are too unstable, fleeting and subjective for this. If we assume, as Sloterdijk does, that architecture is a late maturing of the spontaneous spatial creation of social communities, the sampladelic spatialities can be primarily regarded as proto-architectonic adventures. Dissolving in the sounds of these spatialities – the architecture of the sky – also means dissolving in worlds that continually change in range and size, sound and colour, mood and intensity.

NODAL URBANITY

PART THREE

CHAPTER 1

From Genius to Scenius

THe creative potential of the masses has never been highly acclaimed in Western society. The masses are soon qualified as 'stupid', 'difficult to arouse', and 'not capable of intelligent solutions to complex problems'. The creativity that is championed in Western culture is that of the talented loner. Prior to the fifteenth century, there was only one genius and that was God. This changed when artists in the Renaissance period linked their art to science and articulated their divine capabilities. The idea arose that exceptionally talented individuals such as painters, sculptors and architects were so creative that they could generate an entirely new world. As a result of their knowledge of the central perspective, geometry, anatomy and physiology these artists were able to fathom the inherent laws of creation. They were referred to as 'geniuses' because they possessed a divine madness that elevated them far above the average person.[1]

The current meaning of the concept of 'genius' stretches back to the work of the eighteenth-century German philosopher Immanuel Kant. In the last part of his renowned three *Kritiken*, the *Kritik der Urteilskraft* (Critique of Judgement, 1790), he clearly mentions the idea of genius. To him, a genius is not an elevated or divine being; brilliance is the fruit of a harmonious relationship with one's natural talents. The genius pays attention to what seems to others to be nothing other than coincidence or triviality. He discovers aesthetics in the apparently insignificant. His capability for creativity expresses itself in the unity of his creation, his authenticity is shown by his openness to the smallest details ('*God is in the details*'). To Kant, genius has nothing to do with a talent for an exact simulation of nature. The brilliant artist does not copy nature; in his art, he borrows personal inspiration from the beauty of nature. On this basis, Kant distinguishes between beauty in nature and beauty in art. Art is not a simulation of nature. It presupposes the intervention of the creative human.[2] Art is a product of unbounded creativity that is characterized by an autonomous (autonomy is literally 'self-lawgiving') design. Accordingly, in Kant's view, the genius has a natural talent that can be developed but never acquired.

Since Kant, the genius has become the foundation of every form of originality.[3] This originality comes to the fore in the innovative aspects of the work. We desperately need geniuses for important innovations in science, for new insights in cultural areas, for pioneering achievements in sport. In the past few centuries, the idea of genius has been increasingly strongly connected to the creative individual. The terms 'authenticity' and 'originality' have become synonymous with his personality. With this, the life of a genius has arrived at the focus of attention. A genius is an independent individual who can create a new world out of nothing without having to learn or imitate. His or her rich train of thought is expressed in literature, painting and sculpture, the benchmarks of Western culture. It is this notion of the genius as the creative fundament of our society that has resulted in a long tradition of autobiographies, portraits, and statues.

112]

ALL ALONE IN A GLOBAL WORLD

In the twentieth century, numerous attempts have been made to undermine or deconstruct 'the dark concept of the genius'. Although convincing criticism of the presuppositions at the basis of the prevailing idea of genius have been provided – we only need to refer to Michel Foucault, Gilles Deleuze, and Slavoj Žižek, philosophers who have critiqued the issue of the modernist concept of autonomy – the criticism has not succeeded in reducing the genius's power of attraction to the general public. This coercive fascination also prevails in architecture, where the notion of the genius also plays a major role. To many people, the independent architect with his grand ideas and substantial designs represent the standard for the profession. Who doesn't know the

Guggenheim Museum by Frank Gehry or the Reichstag by Sir Norman Foster? The most striking example is probably Daniel Libeskind, the architect of the Jewish Museum in Berlin and of the new construction at Ground Zero in New York. With his eccentric spectacles, spiky hair, visionary ideas and cowboy boots, he exploits the idea of genius to the full. Peggy Deamer wrote about him in *Perspecta*: *'Seemingly, his depth of thought, enhanced by his reading of philosophy and history, allows him uniquely to perceive the potential of human resources in architectural form; his singularity in this capacity warrants fame. At the same time, he is careful to balance his uniqueness with his accessibility; he must prove that what he sees and feels is what we all see and feel, only deeper.'* [4] Besides Libeskind, other renowned examples of architects who play an increasingly important role in urban design include Frank Gehry, Zaha Hadid, Michael Graves, Phillip Starck, and Rem Koolhaas. They are engaged worldwide in creating an oeuvre that not only consists of buildings but is above all formed by exhibitions and monographs on their ideas, preferences, and tastes.

[113

The notion of the architect as an autonomous artist is even more remarkable because the share of the architect in the design process of museums, football stadiums, offices and airports has actually altered dramatically in the past few years. The classical architect as the person who was responsible for all phases of the design, the budget for the project, the implementation of the plans, and the supervision at the site no longer exists. He fulfils this role only with small-scale assignments, such as those for detached houses. In all other assignments, the architect co-operates with structural engineers, climate consultants, project managers, cost monitors, principals, and advisors in the field of fire safety, sound insulation or façade maintenance. In addition, he has close consultations with government instances in large-scale projects. In an increasing number of projects, the architect is only involved at the beginning of the design process. The details and choice of material for the plan are elaborated by third parties, with the architect and the advisor operating in the background.

AND NOW, ON THE COVER: ARCHITECTS!

Little attention is paid to the fragmentation of the role of the architect. In the description of well-known buildings, the all-important feature is the architect's originality with regard to the design. We relate to a 'celebrity architect' or 'celebrity designer' who hardly exists in real-life practice. The media illusion of the celebrity architect championed by critics, magazines, museums, universities, books and newspapers not only conceals the fact that buildings, streets and squares are created in extremely complex and wide co-operative relationships, the representative model of creativity is also rather obsolete. In popular culture, we can see that extraordinary designs or qualitatively excellent products are also being generated with a completely different form of creativity. Instead of the exceptional talent of the loner, the interactive co-operation between various individuals and parties is more important in this model. The product or design is the result of a dynamic collaboration that is given shape in an exceptional manner.

To cover this co-operative model of co-operation, communication, and information, we introduce the term 'scenius', a word first introduced by the British musician/producer Brian Eno. In a letter to Dave Stewart, a former member of the synth-pop duo Eurythmics, Eno states that important innovations occur when large groups of people co-operate. According to Eno, the scenius stands for the intelligence and intuition of a whole cultural scene. It is the collective form of the genius concept.[5] How can we further describe the scenius? And can the concept be further applied outside the context of pop culture?

If we look at the social-scientific meaning of the concept of 'scene', we can see the contours of the scenius model clearly. Scenius is a combination of the words 'scene' and 'genius'. It combines the horizontal properties of a scene without having recourse to the authenticity and originality of the genius. As such, the word 'genius' is stripped of its strictly individual character. A scene stands for a network of individuals who jointly develop a form of self-styling by means of communication and co-operation. Each scene has a central theme that binds the participants. This may be a music style, a branch of sport, a political idea, an aesthetic tendency, or a sexual preference. Due to its flexible and horizontal character, a scene distinguishes itself from comparable social structures such as gangs, clans, and syndicates. Well-known groups such as Hell's Angels or the Bloods and the Crips – the gangs in Los Angeles – have a strongly hierarchical structure. If one withdraws from this kind of group, this has serious consequences. In contrast to these forms of sociality, a scene creates a low degree of coercion. There are almost no sanctioning measures against the mem-

bers of the scene. Because a scene is not structured on the basis of exclusion, it is not selective. Gender, race or origins are never decisive in
regarding someone as being in or out of a scene.

THE TRAGIC DEATH OF MINER WILLY

In the game industry, the traditional model of the autonomous genius has become obsolete within a relatively short time and has been
replaced by the power of a group of co-operating individuals. In the
realm of computer and video games, the scenius has appeared as a new
model of creativity. In order to understand better this facet of popular culture and to study the extent to which the scenius can be applied
in other practices, the games industry is the ideal starting point for
an analysis. Video games are an important expression of our culture,
which is driven by information and communication. Moreover, the   [115
games industry is one of the fastest-growing sectors of the entertainment industry. As a component of a worldwide economy, its budget is
on a par with that of the film industry in Hollywood. Estimates have
been made that the worldwide turnover in the coming five years will
amount to 100 billion dollars.

To avoid misunderstanding, it can be stated that there are plenty
of geniuses in the popular culture of games. The game *Manic Miner* (Bug Byte, 1983) is a splendid example of a game that was designed
by a nerd in seclusion. The twenty levels of the game were created by
Matthew – '*I call myself an impressionist*' – Smith on one of the first
home computers, the ZX Spectrum. In his mother's home in the English town of Wallasey, the seventeen-year-old Smith conceived, designed, converted to the proper software language all the levels that
Miner Willy must attain, and allocated them suitable music. The technological limitations of the ZX Spectrum, which has a 3.5 MHz proc-
essor, 48 Kb RAM and 16 Kb ROM memory, turned out to be an advantage. Due to the limited possibilities, the talented Smith could develop the game in the isolation of his bedroom.

Only a few years after *Manic Miner*, this kind of design practice
has become inconceivable. Since the early nineties, computer and video games have become the domain of large design teams. The members of the teams are specialized in designing one single component.
The increased power of calculation of the computers and the consoles

on which the games are played are mainly responsible for this much more complex production method. In addition, the enormous amount of work that the production of a game requires can no longer be produced by a loner in his bedroom, regardless of how talented he may be. Even if the next Matthew Smith were to invest several man-years in the development of a new game, the market is developing so rapidly that the game would be immediately out of date. The production costs of a game have become so high that they cannot be raised by one person. At present, creating a new successful title costs between three and five million dollars. As a result of the latest graphic possibilities and the most recent game consoles, the games industry expects that this sum will triple in the coming years.[6]

THE REVOLUTION OF STAR WARS GALAXIES

When the individual designer is replaced by a team of specialists, this does not mean that the production method also radically changes. A group can simply assume the place of the individual author. There is more needed than co-operation between several people to set the scenius in motion. The transition from a talented loner – such as Matthew Smith – to a collective of individuals is only a first, although necessary, step. The second development is the relationship between the game designers and the fans and the users of the game. This ensures that the traditional model of the genius is further relegated to the background. The genesis of *Star Wars Galaxies: An Empire Divided* (Sony, 2001) is an excellent example of the way in which fans and users can become involved in a complex design. In this game, specific methods were developed to make use of the fans and users' knowledge in the design process.

Star Wars Galaxies is a Massively Multiplayer Online Role Playing Game (MMORPG). On the internet, there are many MMORPGs, including *EverQuest* (Sony, 1999) and *World of Warcraft* (Electronic Arts, 1994). In a MMORPG, a large number of people play an online game in a virtual environment which continues to exist even when a player stops playing. Between three and six million people pay a monthly contribution to be able to participate in the online games *Lineage II* (NCsoft, 2004) and *World of Warcraft*. MMORPGs developed from the Multi-User Dungeons (MUDs) that students played at

American universities in the seventies. The extraordinary feature of MUDs was that the players always returned to a shared environment. In the first few years, this environment was primarily textual in its nature. In the course of time, the textual MUDs have changed into comprehensive graphic environments.

To familiarize the general public with *Star Wars Galaxies*, Lucasarts, the company by means of which the director George Lucas wished to add an interactive element to the fantasy world of his films, launched an internet site in conjunction with Sony to announce the issue of the game. The designers not only used the site for the promotion of the game, they also gave gamers an important role in the production. Before the game appeared on the market as a final product, the fans and users were asked for their ideas and comments. By playing the various trial versions and providing comments, these groups were actively involved in the design of their favourite game. This worked both ways. On the one hand, the players could influence the environment of the virtual world in which they would spend hours, days, and even months once the game had been introduced to the market. On the other hand, during the design stages, the designers could benefit from the knowledge and man-hours that the active gamers applied to the product.

The internet site of *Star Wars Galaxies* functioned as a virtual platform that offered the designers the opportunity to put out their feelers toward the community of fans and users. The forum worked as a binding element between the various parties who were interested in the game. Players were no longer approached as dumb consumers and designers were no longer unreachable creators. The role of the designer had become that of an initiator. According to Raph Koster, a fanatic online gamer responsible for the development of *Star Wars Galaxies*, the designers of games are primarily designers of communities: '*Online game design is really a social system design.*'

The starting point for all design activities for a game is the message board. This allows designers to maintain contact with the gamers. This close bond, which the designers or initiators are eager to have with the players, ensures that the latter are closely involved in the game. In the realization of *Star Wars Galaxies*, the initiators introduced a development cycle that consisted of four stages: *in concept, in development, in test,* and *in live*. In the first phase, a new environment, object or character was introduced. In the second stage, new

[117

elements were included in the environment of the game and the consequences of this implementation were studied. In the third stage, these elements were tried and tested. By means of forums, the players could make suggestions about improving various features of the game. The last step was the implementation of the different elements into the game environment.

In this way of working, the role of the initiators was not limited to the introduction of the various designs. It was also their job to keep the game interesting to a large group of users. For this reason, they organized events in the environment of the game. During these events, which normally do not last more than an hour and are supervised by a team of specialists, the players gather at a certain spot in the game environment that is provided by a specific server. These events, which involve finding hidden objects or fighting one another on virtual battlefields, offer the players the opportunity to earn extra points or manpower for the game.

118]

THE SURVIVAL OF THE MOD-EST

The model of the scenius is developing further with the advent of MODs. This abbreviation of the word 'modification' refers to a processing of an original game with new environments, sounds and levels. The vast majority of modifications of existing video games can be found in the genre of action games. In these games, called *First-person Shooter games* (FPS games), the player, with a first person perspective, moves through a three-dimensional space. Behind the barrel of his rifle, he has to shoot as many people and monsters as possible. One of the first three-dimensional FPS games was *Doom*, which was issued by the id Software Company in 1993. *Doom* was the follow-up to *Wolfenstein 3D* (id Software, 1992) in which a player is trapped in a maze with SS soldiers, nasty dogs, and Adolf Hitler. In *Doom*, this historical element was omitted. The horror was reinforced, gunned-down soldiers did not simply vanish but lay there in their own blood. Furthermore, the spatial illusion was more convincing than ever.

Id Software distributed *Doom* by a method that the company referred to as 'shareware'. Players were given the opportunity to download a part of the game from internet, the other levels of *Doom* could be ordered by post after payment. Id Software opted for this alternative distribution method because it could make no use of distributors who ensured that the game lay on the shelves in the shops. Before the games critics even noticed the game, *Doom* was already a major hit in the gamer community due to this shareware method. John Romero, one of the creators of *Doom*, stated: *'We put out a press release in January of 1993 saying what our next game Doom was going to have in it. From January to December, all of 1993, the entire Internet thing was really growing and we had newsgroups about Doom already before the game was out.'* [7]

Doom has an open software structure: the sound and images are stored in separate folders that are freely available to the users. Moreover, the graphic elements of the game can easily be changed according to the wishes of the user. *Doom* initiated an avalanche of modified games that circled on the internet. What was intended as a clever marketing strategy eventually led to countless different versions of the same game.

In 1995, inspired by the success of modifications, the independent publisher D!Zone issued a CD with the nine hundred best, modified versions of *Doom*. The MOD-CD was quickly followed by other titles with the same formula, while other games, such as *Unreal* (GT Interactive, 1998) turned out to be extremely popular as the basic material for other modifications. The game *Red Orchestra: Combined Arms*, in which the players are situated at the Russian front during the Second World War, arose from the futuristic game *Unreal*. The science-fiction décors and the plasma weapons of *Unreal* have made way for realistic images of bombed cities and areas in Russia. Not only have St Petersburg, Feodosia, Sebastopol and the Caucasus been accurately copied, the players also replay historical battles with weapons from the Second World War.

In 1998 the entertainment software company Valve issued the now well-known game *Half-Life*. The modification of this game by a group of students soon after its issue became an enormous success. Research performed by Valve indicates that this version, entitled *TeamFortress* (1998), has been downloaded from internet more than three million times. Valve then decided to buy the game from the students and to put it on the market itself. In the meantime, the company also developed the broadband distribution program Steam in order to inform its players daily of the latest developments. The membership contribution that the players pay when they purchase the game gives them ac-

[119

cess to the internet site where they can download the latest game up-dates. In addition, the site offers enthusiastic MOD makers a chan-nel for the mutual sale of their modifications. In this way, Valve al-lows products of third parties, derived from the original games on its official site. The vigorous trade that has arisen via this channel con-siderably prolongs the lifespan of the original game. This is a big ad-vantage for the distributor of well-known games such as *Half-Life* and *Counterstrike* (Valve, 2004). But there is more: if we compare the way in which people deal with copyrights here in comparison to other sec-tors – we only have to refer to the protective measures applied in the clothing industry, the car industry, and the music sector – we can see that this distribution method is, in the words of the French philoso-pher Alain Badiou, truly revolutionary. Without exaggeration, it can be maintained that this trading style will mean that people outside the games industry will be less and less able to hide behind protec-tionist practices.

120]

Although the number of communities built around game titles is still rather limited, and the complexity of games has increased so strongly that the modification of a game by an individual gamer is be-coming increasingly complicated, the above-described developments show a striking evolution.[8] The production method used in the game culture is diametrically opposed to the traditional model of the gen-ius ('*I did it my way*'). Due to the way in which games are now being created, the standard starting points such as autonomy, originality and authenticity have become open to debate. Not only has the mean-ing of 'creativity' changed, what is being created has also changed. The new item no longer needs to be unique and original. An exist-ing game is consistently reprocessed and, with the application of im-proved techniques and new ideas, can be experienced in a different way. In this process of transformation, the designers have become in-itiators and the players have been allocated the role of the debuggers, scripters, level-builders, and promoters.

IT IS A WIKI'D WORLD

The relationship between the makers and users in the above-men-tioned processes indisputably differs from that in the Fordian produc-tion process in which producers and designers create ready-made objects that roll off the conveyor belts and are presented to the general public by means of advertising campaigns. The scenial producers instigate a communal process in which the manifold products all differ from one another. The games described above have been designed by hundreds, occasionally thousands, of people. The fact that the results are just as good and sometimes even better than those of traditionally-made products is proven by the internet encyclopaedia Wikipedia, which is free and is compiled and maintained by volunteers. The number of articles in the English-language version has now surpassed the million mark. An average of seventeen hundred articles are added daily to this reference work. As a result, this encyclopaedia is not only larger than Encyclopaedia Britannica – the most important rival maintained by professional staff – the articles are also similar in accuracy.[9]

What are the dynamics of the scenius? In the scenius, the intelligence of a large group of individuals is mobilized and made productive. This does not just occur as a matter of course; it is essential to have a structure or model within which the parties involved can make their contribution. To make the scenius model operational, we can distinguish three groups: initiators, fans, and users. These form the foundation of the scenius. [121

The initiators launch the project by setting the creative process in motion. This process is picked up by fans and users over the entire world. The initiators are the apostles of their own product. They translate specific and technological knowledge into images, films, manuals or test environments in order to make these comprehensible and to give fans and users a share in design decisions. By sharing the knowledge and information present, the product can constantly change. The exchange of information and knowledge is not a chain of causality but rather of simultaneity. The more people who are aware of a game, the greater the chance that the product can be improved. Each change within this production circle can lead to innovations that again lead to an increase in communal knowledge and information.

At the centre of the scenius we find the fans who are frequently so involved in the process that they have little interest in anything else. Although they may often be placed in a disparaging light, the fans play a positive role in the scenius. This negative appraisal lurks in the word 'fan', which is an abbreviation for the Latin word 'fanaticus' literally meaning 'of or belonging to a temple, a temple servant, a devotee'. At the same time, the concept is associated with an obsessive commitment to a political or religious matter. At the end of the nineteenth century, the term came into fashion in America as a name for enthusiastic baseball supporters. Later the term was applied to describe those who closely followed pop culture.[10] Nonetheless, the word has never really lost its negative connotation. The fans, just like the Japanese *Hikikomori*, are often approached in a deprecating manner. They are occasionally called 'mindless consumers' or 'social misfits' who waste their lives on useless things and attach too much importance to inferior expressions of culture. Because they are not capable of distinguishing between fantasy and reality, the fans are often seen as being childish and intellectually immature.[11] In the film *The Fan* (1996) fans are even associated with deranged psychopaths and stalkers. In this blockbuster, Robert De Niro plays an extremely obsessed fan who will do anything to help his idol, the baseball player Bobby Rayburn, overcome his form crisis.

122]

In *Textual Poachers*, the American media theorist Henry Jenkins argues that the clarification and interpretation of texts should not only be the responsibility of writers and academics. According to Jenkins, the fans of popular television series such as *Star Trek* or *The Beauty and the Beast* are just as capable of taking significance from all kinds of established and less establish cultural expressions: '*Unimpressed by institutional authority and expertise, the fans assert their own right to form interpretations, to offer evaluations, and to construct cultural canons. Undaunted by traditional conceptions of literary and intellectual property, fans raid mass culture, claiming its materials for their own use, reworking them as the basis for their own cultural creations and social interactions.*'[12] It is striking that the fans lack all academic or literary distance. To them, the traditional distinction between popular and 'high' culture is irrelevant. The fans embrace commercial entertainment and appropriate story lines and ideas in a completely self-evident manner. Because pop culture is inextricably linked to their own lives, they want to have a say in the storyline, the characters, and the appearance of the main actors.

In the vortex of the scenius, the fans manifest themselves on internet platforms, at conventions and meetings. They create their own communal language and interactive style. Inasmuch as their daily work allows it, the fans spend all their time on affective networking. To them, the scenius is much more than a leisure time activity. It is a way of thinking and living. In this respect, the fans distinguish themselves from the final users. Not only do fans spend much more time on the generation of the product, they also know more, so that they understand the nuances and the mutual references much better. Nevertheless, not all fans are part of the scenius. That only occurs when they manifest themselves as a group and make their knowledge widely available.

The third group within the scenius is that of the users. Just like the fans, the users are the consumers of the producers. As more consumers arrive on the scene, the fans become more important. But whereas the fans, with their specific knowledge, close themselves off from other knowledge areas, the users are seeking change and combinations with other spheres and cultures. The users place the product in the world, give it a position next to all the other products, and establish contact with other users. They represent the most open aspect of the scenius.

[123

THE EMPOWERMENT OF CREATIVITY

The mainspring of the scenius is the interaction between the initiators, the fans and the users. Not only are new services and products generated by means of the intensive co-operation of these three parties, but new mutual relationships are also forged. The exceptional form of communication brings with it new words and an own distinct use of language. A flexible, social structure, in which the role of the various groups blurs, is formed around the product. In the scenius, the three groups constantly influence one another. Each user can become a fan and, in turn, the fans can assume the position of the initiators. Moreover, the initiators often belong to the most enthusiastic users. Don't the philosophers Hardt and Negri also speak of the scenius when they claim in their book *Multitude*, in which they hold a powerful plea for a radical-democratic form of productive co-operation, that: *'We have to rid ourselves of the notion that innovation relies on the genius of an individual. We produce and innovate together only in networks. If there is an act of genius, it is the genius of the multitude'*? [13]

The question arises as to whether the scenius model can be applied to the design of the city, of buildings, streets and squares. If we examine the way in which residents and users of buildings or urban quarters are now involved in the design process, it quickly becomes evident that their influence rarely extends further than a restricted form of participation. Urban planners and architects present their plans to residents via an internet site or public-discussion evenings. Occasionally the residents are allowed to choose from a limited number of designs, or can articulate their preferences on details such as the colour of the façades, the street lighting, or the greenery in the neighbourhood. The maximum involvement that is asked of the residents is that they make a choice, where the majority of votes determines the decision. A problem in this form of involvement is that every form of hierarchy is lacking. Regardless of their degree of knowledge, commitment or involvement, all the residents and users have an equal say. As a result, people are not encouraged to study the topic, let alone identify with it, as fans do in a different context. The vortex that we observed previously in the production of computer games is completely absent in this process, due to the few opportunities that the users have of applying their influence.

124]

When we contrast this form of involvement with the ideas of Eric Raymond, it becomes obvious just how obsolete and worn-out this co-operation has become. In *The Cathedral and the Bazaar*, Raymond distinguishes between two production models for the development of software.[14] In the first model – the cathedral model – a limited number of people write the consecutive versions of the software. If this meets their requirements, the product is placed on the market. Raymond recognizes many disadvantages of working this way, certainly in comparison to the second model, which he refers to as the 'bazaar model'. In this method, the software is developed in such a way that it can be improved by everyone. When the attention and power of thought of an entire community can be maintained, this leads to the best result, according to Raymond. The foundation of the open source projects of the bazaar model is the realization that creating a design is a self-evolving process in which the wishes of fans and users must be taken into account

'Who conceived or realized this work?' and 'What does the author wish to express in his work?' are the questions pertinent to the one-to-many model. Different questions are asked in the many-to-many model of the scenius: 'What is the reach of the work? In which other places is the work also used? Is there scope for other authors and where is that scope?' For the design of buildings, urban quarters, streets and squares, the scenius would have consequences that can scarcely be overestimated. In that model, the designers should not solely devote their attention to the artistic or ultimate product. They ought to accommodate and establish co-operative structures that harmonize with the many-to-many model in order to realize important changes and innovations in a new manner.

AND SUDDENLY THERE IS THE NETWORK

Think in terms of networks and everything changes into a network. Biologists refer to the diversity of the natural ecosystem of animals as the 'food networks'. Worldwide, several thousand radical Muslims form part of terrorist networks. And systems whose composition is derived from the way in which human brains work are called 'neural networks'. A network consists of points, connections and relationships. It can assume one of three forms: central, decentral, and distributed. In a central network, all the different points are linked via one nucleus. The points are not connected to one another but are linked because they converge at one central point. If this central hub vanishes, the network dissolves into detached points. A decentral network is a multiple of the central network: the hubs are linked to one another and with the smaller points. In the third form – the distributed network – there is no hierarchy among the points. All the points are connected with several and partly varying points so that a diversity of connections is generated. Even if certain points vanish, the distributed network continues to function until a certain critical limit is reached.

[125

The many-to-many scenius model is an example of a distributed network. Does this kind of approach have any chance of success in the context of architecture? This means that in the planning process for buildings, streets and squares, the emphasis shifts from the design of tangible objects to social processes. The design process begins with the forging of alliances with the residents, interested parties, project developers, and government authorities. In this way, a similar synergy can arise as is found among users, fans and initiators in the game industry. In the meantime, there are various examples of co-operative efforts between the government and private parties to exchange knowledge and information. These are mainly entered into in large-scale projects to restrict the financial risks to a minimum. The construction of the centre of the Dutch city Almere is an excellent example of this. Almere was built because there was a huge demand for family houses with a garden in the vicinity of Amsterdam. The architect Rem Koolhaas referred to the method by means of which the centre plan for Almere was elaborated as the 'Japanese model'. This model is characterized by much discussion, where nobody negotiates to the extreme. By a process of give and take, the plan ultimately develops to the satisfaction of all.[15]

This Japanese model suggests an open process in which communication is an essential element for arriving at a workable design. This form of co-operation can also be compared to the scenius model with the qualification that the Japanese model still involves a closed group. The knowledge and man-hours of possible residents and other users are not mobilized in any way whatsoever. Communication only occurs between architects, government authorities, and project developers. A genuine democratization of the process, so that a design gains broad general support and can be embedded in the physical and social space of the city, does not occur here. In a 'democratic process', a designer is a part of a widespread network in which he accommodates, processes and advances the knowledge of the users and opens the plan to improvement. By optimizing the connections, he maintains the momentum of the vortex of the scenius or communal commitment.[16]

126]

SMART MASSES

When 'the masses' genuinely receive a share in the design, the issue inevitably arises concerning whether or not this will lead to worthless and ugly results. The German artist Jörg Immendorff answers his own rhetorical question: 'If I hold a referendum on what should be presented in the museums, what would be shown there?' with one word: 'Rubbish!' Apparently we encounter fundamental doubts on this topic. However, it is too easy to claim that processes such as the scenius have no underlying structure and therefore lead to dramatic results. The opposite is true. The scenius is not a free play of forces, it cannot function without a form of order or regulation. It is a myth that the scenius is an open realm of spontaneous and autonomous forces that can act without any form of control and sanctions. If we wanted to apply the scenius model to designing the physical environment, it is absolutely necessary that the initiators establish coherent, sober and selective supervision to guide the dynamic processes in the right direction. The development cycle of *Star Wars Galaxies* is an excellent example of this. The developmental cycle consisted of fixed moments at which the fans and users could offer comments and could make improvements to the three-dimensional environments in the game. Until the moment that the game was definitively brought into operation, this cycle ensured that the contributions from these groups became increasingly refined. A certain degree of elitism played a major role in this process.

With the intention of allocating residents more say in the layout of their living environment, the Antillean architect Carel Weeber introduced the idea of 'free living' into the Netherlands.[17] Weeber proposed taking the 'supervision' of physical space away from planners and architects and giving residents a greater voice in the design of their own homes. To ensure that bad taste and a lack of variation would not dominate, Weeber suggested providing an extensive catalogue of possibilities from which people could choose the house of their dreams. Although Weeber claims that the users ought to be of the utmost importance, he makes a critical error here. Not only does the design of the physical environment remain in the hands of the planners, the design is not based in any way on the demands, yearnings, and criteria of the users themselves. The scenius model indicates that it is possible to formulate specific goals to which all the relevant parties orient their efforts. This means that it is not the components of the catalogue that ought to be designed but rather the process in which a high-quality, pragmatic catalogue can arise. On this basis, people from outside the field of architecture can also make a valuable contribution.

[127

Another precondition of the innovative power of the scenius is the fact that screened-off knowledge areas become accessible. For the exchange of knowledge, it is not only necessary that existing work and ideas be less stringently protected by author's rights, copyrights and patents, they should also be made available for re-interpretation. Only then can knowledge that is inaccessible due to all kinds of forms of specialization and privatization be shared. Even more importantly, the coercive mechanism of design competitions in the realm of architecture ought to be re-examined. As a result of European regulations, which oblige governments to organize open tenders for assignments with a fee of 200,000 Euro and more, open or limited architectural competitions are being arranged increasingly frequently for the design of government buildings. Although these rules prevent the assignments repeatedly going to the same architects, there are also considerable disadvantages in this system. In an architectural competition, a small group of involved persons formulate the brief, the level of ambition, and the available budget for the construction of a theatre, museum, residential area, or urban quarter. Subsequently, a jury is charged with the responsibility of assessing the plans submitted and of determining which design is to be implemented. A good example of this practice is the competition organized in 2003 for the construction of the Grand Egyptian Museum in Giza. The open architectural competition attracted 1557 submissions, from 83 different countries. Eventually the design submitted by Heneghan Peng Architects was chosen. Thus, only one design from the many hundreds remained. This practice of distributing assignments excludes any far-reaching co-operation and development of ideas between the participants. Every participant is asked to think about the same problem, but after the winner has been chosen, the knowledge and ideas of the other partici-

128] pants are left redundant. In addition, the principals choose a specific design or a favourite style and not a plan of action.

THE SCENIUS: MORE IS MORE

This chapter witnessed the introduction of the concept of 'scenius', a combination of the words 'scene' and 'genius'. The scenius champions the open dynamics of the group and puts into perspective the significance of authenticity and originality, values which accompany the alleged superiority of the individual. One of the most important characteristics of the scenius is the co-operation between the initiators, the fans and the users who gather around a shared interest or a specific goal. The interaction between these three parties is the motivating force behind this many-to-many model. The most striking feature of the scenius is the fact that it breaks with the traditional one-to-many model that is closely linked to the notion of the individual genius. The scenius demands more interaction from the participants than the classical one-to-many principle where there is a passive form of consumption.

We may be accused of being too optimistic about the possibilities of the scenius and it may be debatable whether or not a concept from pop culture can be applied without reservation in another domain. Accordingly, a warning is justified here. To tackle the spatial problems and challenges of the city, an instrumental approach to the scenius would be too simple. It would then be regarded as a neutral and value-free instrument that can be applied to any random domain to deal with new challenges. This kind of approach pays no attention to the positive and negative properties of this specific 'invention' of popular culture. In addition, it ignores the fact that certain problems cannot be detached from the changes in urban space that we described in the previous chapter. People too often lose sight of the fact that developments are not isolated occurrences. Technological, military, financial and political changes are closely related and have a great impact on the layout and experience of the urban space in our society.

People may regard us as naïve or short-sighted. Due to its unpredictability and complexity, the process of the layout of physical space cannot be compared to the design of other spatialities such as the virtual space of *Star Wars Galaxies* or the sonic space of the techno. But is the substantiation of a virtual spatiality really nothing more than a one-dimensional happening? Is the generation of a coherent sonic spatiality truly such a simple process? There will be good reasons why the many-to-many model of the scenius has not been enthusiastically emulated; the observation itself is remarkable. After all, the scenius offers various footholds for dealing with the design of the physical space of the city in a different manner. As we have seen, the model can be used as a concrete proposal for working on the layout of urban space. One simple suggestion: more parties, different techniques, new solutions. [129

Whatever reservations people may have about the scenius, no one can deny that, in contrast to urban planners and architects, people in the popular games culture have succeeded in creating a coherent social structure in the design of large-scale environments. Not only does the role of the architect acquire new substantiation in the scenius model, but the position of parties such as the project developers and the government authorities will also change in character and content. It will be up to the initiators (principals, government authorities, technological advisors, etc.) to launch a communal process in conjunction with the users. No longer will the aesthetic or the beautiful be the driving force behind the design process, nor will everything be oriented toward the exceptional qualities of the individual genius. The greatest challenge of the design process is democratization. Only due to the alliance of initiators, users and fans the common can genuinely become the focus of attention.

CHAPTER 2

The City in a Flooded World

UNtil now we have only spoken of mediascapes, the flows of expression of popular culture. In his book *Modernity at Large*, Arjun Appadurai distinguishes, besides the mediascapes, four other flows or movements that are a part of the globalization process: *ethnoscapes* (worldwide ethnic networks), *technoscapes* (worldwide technological infrastructures), *financescapes* (networks of capital flows), and *ideoscapes* (ideologies of national states and action groups). In Appadurai's opinion, these flows cross, influence and reinforce one another at world level. In this way, the new communication possibilities of the technoscapes contribute greatly to people leaving their homelands. The images and stories of the mediascapes also influence the movements of immigrants, tourists and foreign workers. On this point, Appadurai emphasizes the impact of popular mass media such as games, music and film. He writes: *'The imagination is now central to all forms of agency, is itself a social fact, and is the key component of the new global order.'*[18]

In this concluding chapter, we focus on the influence of popular culture from the mediascapes on the thought patterns covering the city. To unravel the complexity of urban space and to obtain a better grasp of the diversity of ideas from popular culture, we describe a body of four differentiated, mutually influential processes that permeate the urban space: virtuality, interactivity, connectivity, and multimediality. This complex of processes is given shape in what we refer to as 'nodal urbanity'. This concept implies two important changes in comparison to a more traditional form of urbanity. As a consequence of the way in which these four processes of virtuality, interactivity, connectivity and multimediality resonate in our own lives, there is no longer mention of an urbanity that is identical everywhere. The process of urbanization does not conform to universal laws and fixed patterns. Instead, we approach the city as a relational and contextual entity, rather than as a material fixed quality. Urbanity can be subject to a different substantiation at every different place. What are the consequences for the determination of physical space? Which social problems and challenges does nodal urbanity involve? At the same time, we must not lose sight of a second change. Besides the metamorphosis of the physical space, a gradual change in the way we deal with that new space is also occurring. The influence of the above-mentioned processes on our direct environment also causes changes in the way we experience ourselves and our direct environment.

[131

WHAT'S THE BIG DEAL WITH METAPHORS?

In order to form a precise picture of the changes that are taking place in the field of urbanity, we should not regard urbanization as an independent, purely physical phenomenon.[19] Immaterial movements such as mediascapes are also determining factors in our experience of urbanity. Virtuality is an important component of this. Although various writers have devoted attention to the dimension of the virtual environment, only a few have covered the virtual character of the images and information from the popular media. Just how complicated the issue of virtuality actually is when dealing with the city becomes clear when the architecture of the virtual space is put into words. The description of virtual spatiality makes use of terms such as 'a space without a centre' or 'sprawl of hubs'. Vice versa, the analysis of our everyday living environment often makes use of classical terms like the 'web', 'matrix', 'grid', or 'field'. From this rather unclear perspective, Marcos Novak, who refers to himself as a 'trans-architect', introduced the term 'liquid architecture'. In this context, Novak speaks of a fourth dimension. In doing so, he signifies a fluid, imaginary landscape that only exists in a virtual world formed by information and communications processes. This architecture, which owes its existence to the computer technology used in the design process, is not impeded by gravity and other tedious problems with which architects struggle when they build in a 'real' environment where walls can sag and roofs may leak. In the fourth dimension not only time and space but also form and structure are assigned a different embedding.

This description of the changes at urban level may be too limited and one-sided. The physical world is reduced to a number of metaphors borrowed from virtuality, and vice versa, the virtual world is characterized in terms of physical space. Manuel Castells also seems to be guilty of this practice when, in his monumental work *The Information Age*, he refers to the first layer of the virtual circuit – that of the 'space of flows', where he situates the electronic exchange of capital, information, images, sounds, and symbols – as a spatial domain: *'Thus, it is a spatial form, just as it could be "the city" or "the region" in the organization of the merchant society or of the industrial society.'* [20]

132]   Thus, two types of metaphors dominate the terminology. One the one hand, we encounter metaphors that refer to virtual reality in terms of physical space, whereas, on the other, there are metaphors that describe physical reality in virtual terms, where there is a flirt with the idea that we find ourselves in a world that is held together by bits, bytes, images, wires, and electronic streams.

Let us begin with the normative metaphors for virtual spatiality. The most frequent spatial appellation of the virtual dimension is 'cyberspace' and the 'electronic highway'. The term 'cyberspace' was first used by the sci-fi writer William Gibson. In his book *Neuromancer*, he sketched the environment of a computer matrix that has no connection with tangible reality. To Gibson, cyberspace is a hallucinatory space that unfolds when the brain is directly linked to a worldwide network of computers. He writes: *'A consensual hallucination experienced daily by billions of legitimate operators, in every nation, by children being taught mathematical concepts ... A graphical representation of data abstracted from the banks of every computer in the human system. Unthinkable complexity. Lines of light ranged in the non-space of the mind, clusters and constellations of data. Like city lights, receding .... .'* [21] To reinforce the metaphor of the virtual information network, Gibson refers to Los Angeles. When Gibson thinks of cyberspace, he recalls the satellite photo of this city by night.

The extent to which the fixation on the physical space can reach in the description of a virtual dimension is shown by John Perry Barlow, one of the founders of the *Electronic Frontier Foundation*. In his *Cyberspace Declaration of Independence*, Barlow reacts to the proposals of the American government to censure the internet by means of the *Telecommunications Reform Act*. To Barlow, there is only one option: the proclamation of the independence of cyberspace. After the Declaration of Independence of the United States, a next step must be made; after all, the independence of cyberspace is under threat. In Barlow's vision, the virtual world of internet ought to be cleansed of every form of regulation by the national state. More specifically, it ought to remain beyond the grasp of the American government. In his manifesto, Barlow describes the virtual dimension in the same terms as physical space is also depicted: *'Governments of the Industrial World, you weary giants of flesh and steel, I come from Cyberspace, the new home of the Mind. On behalf of the future, I ask you of the past to leave us alone. You are not welcome among us. You have no sovereignty where we gather. (...) I declare the global social space we are building to be naturally independent of the tyrannies you seek to impose on us. (...) Cyberspace does not lie within your borders. (...) This governance will arise according to the conditions of our world, not yours. Our world is different. (...) We will create a civilization of the Mind in Cyberspace.'* [22]   [133

The use of spatial metaphors does not limit itself to the virtual world. The second type of metaphor clothes the physical environment in a virtual coat. The global village of Marshall McLuhan is the most renowned example. In his book *The Gutenberg Galaxy*, he states: *'The new electronic interdependence recreates the world in the image of a global village.'* [23] With the paradoxical term 'global village' he refers to the explosive growth of electronic media, which – according to McLuhan – make the world a coherent whole and generate a feeling of great involvement among all the inhabitants: *'The electro-magnetic discoveries have recreated the simultaneous "field" in all human affairs so that the human family now exists under conditions of a "global village".'* Although the term global village initially referred to the changes that occurred after the advent of television, the metaphors seems to be truly applicable with the upsurge of other media from the mediascapes, such as online games like *World of Warcraft* and *Lineage II*. In these synthetic worlds, the registered players live under an avatar – the representation of a player in a shared virtual world – in environments they have built themselves. Estimates indicate that, every day, between eleven and twelve million people occupy these parallel worlds that only exist on servers in the United States, Europe or South Korea. In these global villages, players co-operate, attempt to accumulate wealth in the form of weapons and property, and even marry one another. To give lustre to these weddings, various MMORPGs offer suitable locations, festive clothing, and wedding rings.

THE CITY IN A LAPTOP

The advantage of metaphors is that they make the unknown more comprehensible by means of a recognizable picture. The metaphor is thus a proven means of making new developments accessible. In the theory-forming on the modern city, much use, albeit perhaps extremely one-sided, was made of the idea that present-day developments in the field of urbanity can be analysed by comparing them to virtual processes. The book *City of Bits* by William Mitchell is an excellent example of this. In this, Mitchell describes the city as a collection of virtual networks: a digital gathering of electronic data. This gives rise to the image of a city that is plugged into an invisible spatiality that consists of many virtual spaces which are interconnected by information and communication processes.[24] In Mitchells' view, the effect of these virtual processes on the materialized form of the city is so great that a new type of spatiality is generated. This reasoning of cause and effect echoes more clearly when he predicts that various kinds of buildings will change in form under the influence of virtual processes. He believes that the primary function of museums, theatres, schools, prisons, universities, and shops will change radically when these buildings are embedded in a virtual infrastructure: *'Buildings and parts of buildings must now be related not only to their natural and urban contexts, but also to their cyberspace settings.'* [25]

On the basis of its technological determinism, in which virtual networks govern how we live and work, the virtual immaterial space assumes the place of the physical space: *'Soon, all the world will be in an electronic stage.'* [26] The city remains locked up in Mitchell's laptop. And thus the circle is complete: the virtual extends into the physical and the physical shrinks as a result of the virtual. *'Buildings will be computer interfaces and computer interfaces will become buildings.'* [27] Mitchell's vision is based on the naïve optimism that the virtual space

134]

of flows will also largely remove the discomforts and frictions we experience in everyday reality. Moreover, he claims that, in his laptop, the city will be rid of every form of regulation, control, or exercise of power. The result of this approach is that ultimately no distinction can be made between the virtual and the physical urban environment. They will have become one another's mirror image. In the first part of *The Information Age*, Castells warns for this disruption of functions. In contrast to Mitchell, Castells maintains that schools and universities will scarcely dissolve into a virtual spatiality. Although it is no longer possible to imagine a classroom without a computer, these institutions will be the least influenced by the virtual 'space of flows'. Besides the provision of education, schools also increasingly fulfil other functions such as the extra-mural care of children. And at universities, too, the face-to-face interaction with students will remain a necessary element in education.[28]

Despite these nuances, it remains a fact that the antithesis between virtual and tangible reality has become less clear-cut with the embedding of physical space in a virtual dimension. At the same time, it cannot be emphasized enough that we ought not to allow ourselves to conclude that there is no longer a distinction between a space relying on computer networks and physical space. This would not only mean that the city had lost its bond with material reality, but also that the difference between 'true' and 'fictive' has disappeared. The French philosopher Jean Baudrillard seems to have succumbed to the seduction of the virtual when he claims that we are living in a hyperreality of codes and simulations. He uses the term 'simulacrum' to describe this concept of a copy of a copy with which there is no longer any correspondence in reality. The principal problem with this manner of thinking, in which appearance and truth converge, is that we can no longer formulate concrete action perspectives to give life form and content.

A more convincing elucidation of the distinction between reality and virtuality can be found in Christine Boyer's analysis of the influence of media virtuality in her book *CyberCities*. Without giving way to euphoria, she describes the city as a complex chessboard of *plug-in* zones and suburbs that are connected by an extensive network of motorways, telephones, computer banks, glass fibre cables, radio, and television. In Boyer's view, a cyber city is forming in front of our eyes, under our feet, above our heads: '*This unwieldy mixture of cyber-*

*space and urban dystopia – here called CyberCities – turns the reality
of time and place into an imaginary matrix of computer nets electron-
ically linking together distant places around the globe and communi-
cating multilinearly and consequentially with vast assemblages of information stored as electronic codes.'* [29] To her, the fact that daily life
is permeated with the virtual does not mean the end of the city, as it
does to Mitchell. This leads, at most, to the fact that we can no longer define the city primarily in terms of fixed, geographical boundaries. Wasn't that something we also encountered in the architecture
of Archigram, Detroit's techno, and the youth culture Urban?

In addition, Boyer concluded that the use of metaphors is less innocent than might appear at first sight. She warns for the danger that metaphors change our perception and influence the forming of knowledge
on the city. Boyer rightly claims that *'there is a tendency to impose
the synthetic purity of cyberspace on real urban space and only fill in
the hubs of the matrix'.*[30] In Boyer's view, the use of metaphors leads
to the misunderstanding that the leap from virtual to physical space
– from the virtual matrix to the physical urban space – can be made
without too much difficulty. The analogy between the electronic matrix of cyberspace – in the fictive meaning of a power-free environment – and a concrete urban space can cause a dangerous phenomenon.
According to Boyer, in the metaphorical leap in which the physical environment is put on a par with the virtual world, it is *'no more than
logical to exclude the intervening space of degeneration, alienation,
and silence from the grid.'*[31] It is no coincidence that this intervening
space is currently inhabited by drop-outs and the living dead of our
society: junkies, beggars, the homeless. In this context, Boyer refers
to the 'safe zones' in Miami, which lie well out of sight of the city residents.[32] These are the places that those homeless and addicts have been
allocated by the city council for eating, sleeping, and washing without
running the risk of being immediately arrested by security services.

[136]

POP-UP CITIES

The metaphors of the virtual function as a conceptual filter. However, this entails the danger that urban space might be defined as a ster-
ile environment, free of every stain. The untidy shadow sides of life
converge in what Castells calls 'the black holes of informational cap-

italism'. Instead of attempting to capture urban space in a definition that claims to have general validity, it is more productive to describe the four mediascape processes that influence the generation of various forms of urbanity. These processes can then be taken as the basis of an analysis of how they not only restructure our immediate environment but also ensure that we experience this environment in a new manner.

Until now we have only discussed the ubiquity of the virtual and its actualization in everyday reality. However, virtuality is not the only immaterial process that exerts influence on the city. Besides virtuality there are other processes that shape or influence urban space. To understand the changes that are occurring all around us, we also have to take these processes into account. The genesis of other forms of urbanity will be related to the complex processes in the mediascapes as well as the media that form the basis of these. Besides virtuality, we can also distinguish multimediality, connectivity, and [137 interactivity. These are the four different components of the genetic coding of a form of urbanity that we call 'nodal'. Nodal urbanity is the name of a coherent urban life that is no longer defined in purely physical terms.

1 *Virtuality*. Manuel Castells observed that the territory of the city is not solely determined by physical space. The virtuality of various movements or networks also plays an important role in the factor of spatiality. When certain regions, cities and territories are not embedded in the virtual space of flows, they become, as Castells puts it, stripped of the technological infrastructure that is necessary to communicate, innovate, produce, consume; in short, to live in a larger worldly context. From the perspective of the global information economy, these cities or areas no longer have economic value. What happens with, for example, an area that has not been included in a Tom-Tom navigation system? Such cities or areas are no more than a tourist curiosity or a refuge for stressed-out managers who retreat without a mobile phone or laptop.

It is necessary to acknowledge that this form of virtuality can only function because it has a spatial manifestation. To indicate this spatial entity, Saskia Sassen points to well-known *Global Cities*. Cities such as Tokyo, London and New York form the most important hubs in the current worldwide information economy. This has the important consequence for the physical space that the notion of virtuality also leads to changes in the scale, speed and patterns of the process of urbanization. The financial districts of Wall Street in New York and The City in London assume their own strategic positions because they have been partly detached from their direct environments. Their position is no longer primarily linked to the ground they occupy. Because they are embedded in a widespread network, Global Cities can no longer be reduced to a specific area of ground as a part of a state. A different spatial geography has taken over, a translocal network of global cities that is, in Sassen's opinion, equally sharply delineated and structured.[33]

The power of the virtual extends further than the trade in shares and obligations. Other virtual environments are also popping up in the 'real' world. A parallel economy has arisen around MMORPGs such as *EverQuest* and *Ultima Online* (Electronic Arts, 1997) in which the goods and attributes used in these games, such as houses, weapons, costumes and characters, are traded for thousands of dollars on special auctions sites like MyGameStock and Internet Game Exchange. If one searches eBay with the term 'online games', one uncovers a virtual economy that is equal to the gross national product of an average African country. In 2001, the American economist Edward Castronova, who researched Norrath – the virtual environment of the online role game *EverQuest* – concluded that the economy of this game is the seventy-seventh largest economy in the world. As such, it is situated between the economies of Russia and Bulgaria.

Where is this process of virtualization leading us? In May 2006, the makers of the game *Project Entropia* (MindArk AB, 2004) announced that the virtual money in this online game can be issued as 'real' money at special cash dispensers. Ten Project Entropia Dollars (P.E.D.) are worth the same as one American dollar. Things like fraud and theft are also no longer the exclusive privilege of normal 'reality'. According to a report formulated by the South Korean police, online gamers are increasingly becoming the target of criminals. In 2002, South Korea witnessed forty thousand reports of computer crime. That is eighteen per cent up on the previous year. More than half of the registrations involved crime in relation to online games. Swindlers offered virtual, stolen, game money for sale in the real world. In the virtual world of games, the South Korean police distinguishes between three forms of crime: hacking someone else's access codes to steal game attributes, the theft of online identities of other players, and fraud with the sale of virtual game attributes on internet.[34] One of the major fraud cases led to the arrest of two Korean hackers. They broke into a game server in order to gain a considerable amount of virtual money which they later sold to other gamers. In this way, the two criminals managed to acquire almost a million Euro. To counteract the great number of thefts of virtual attributes from online games, the South Korean police has now set up a police unit that is specialized in this form of crime.

2   *Multimediality*. The city is a melting pot of media that interact with one another. Whereas Times Square in New York was once the example *par excellence* of a place that was flooded by images, analogous and digital pictures now compete with one another on every street corner. Metres-high screens display the latest adverts for Calvin Klein and Levi's, gigantic television screens and illuminated bulletin boards inform passers-by of the latest news and weather forecasts. Long before a car has reached its destination, news boards inform the drivers that there are still tickets available for the concert that evening, or that there is parking space in the nearest car park, and how many seconds it will take before the traffic light at the exit for the car park will turn green. And these are only the digital signs. The images and slogans on billboards, posters, graffiti and stickers on walls, letterboxes, buses and traffic lights all vie with one another for attention. The city has become the stage for overlapping and mutually referring media. [139

According to Boyer, this gathering of images and information has placed the classical concept of 'the city' under pressure and it is becoming increasingly difficult to form a concrete representation of the city. Los Angeles and Tokyo have become literally inconceivable: '*In the end, this flood of images of the city fails to offer the spectator a stable sense of physical reality, because public space appears impermanent and nondescript within the persistent flow of information. Thus perception of the physical city begins to shift. We divert our eyes tot protect ourselves from the tyranny of constant visualisation.*'[35] As a consequence, we regard the city as a combination of various media: a multimedia compilation of text, image, movement and sound, rather than as a delineated, territorial unit. At an analytical level, the city differs little from popular media such as video games in which moving pictures, sound and texts are fused into a unique whole. While playing an action game, a player is confronted with deafening sounds, speaking action figures, and a realistic presentation of urban spatialities. One only needs to recall previously-mentioned war games such as *Delta Force: Black Hawk Down*, which include recorded film and television pictures of the conflict in Mogadishu, Somalia.[36] The unique feature of the city is that it has now become a bastard environment itself in which everything is continually being transformed and medialized. The physical environment is a hybrid location in which various spatialities merge with one another. In short, the city itself has become a mass medium.[37]

3 *Connectivity.* The fact that urbanity is not only rooted in the physical but can also be regarded from a virtual and multimedia point of view offers scope for a third process, that of connectivity. A nodal point only functions when it is embedded in multiple processes via a series of different connections. A city not only extends in a horizontal direction (motorways, railway lines, suburbs) and a vertical direction (skyscrapers, transmission masts). Independently of this physical extension, an urban environment concretizes itself also in the convergence of the four mediascape processes. Which social hubs are generated in these flows? How are those hubs actualized in everyday reality? By connectivity, we are referring to the way in which media processes enable people throughout the world to link up with one another and enter into social relationships. In his book *The Virtual Community*, Howard Rheingold defines virtual communities as follows: '*Social aggregations that emerge from the Internet when enough people carry on public discussions long enough and with sufficient human feeling to form webs of personal relationships in cyberspace.*' In reality, however, virtual communities with a strong mutual bond are rather rare. It is better to speak of thin communities in which people tend to remain strangers and are not aware of one another's true gender, name, or age.[38]

Nevertheless, we wish to apply the term connectivity to indicate that a social environment can develop within the popular media. '*It's not gaming, it's socializing.*' We demonstrated that in the previous chapter with the scenius, which actively involves gamers in the design of environments for new computer games. Apart from this close involvement, connectivity also offers the possibility for several people to participate in a game simultaneously by means of a network model. On the basis of subscription costs, millions of players from all kinds of countries are active in the virtual environment of the MMORPGs,

140]

such as *Lineage II* and *World of Warcraft*. The social reality that thus arises develops independently of historical or geographical links and is completely saturated with a popular culture spanning the entire world. Accordingly, connectivity ought to be regarded as a deterritorialized system of social relations. Connectivity gives rise to a mediaspora of public spheres or places where a society is formed, which could also be referred to as 'virtual neighbourhoods'. What makes connectivity genuinely innovative is the fact that this communality spreads out worldwide. The result is a network to which all one-way traffic is alien. With the electronic globalization of pop culture, a community that continually changes in size, place and character unfolds.

4   *Interactivity*. While the effects of virtuality, multimediality, and connectivity are not the cause of great discussion, there is a true difference of opinion on the definition and value of the concept of interactivity. Everyone agrees that it is a container concept. Many critics wonder if it actually adds anything to our comprehension of the working of the media. According to Espen Aarseth, the founder of the cybertext theory, interactivity is nothing other than a trendy word, a cheap rhetorical trick of industry to stimulate more turnover: '*The industrial rhetoric produced concepts such as interactive newspapers, interactive video, interactive television, and even interactive houses, all implying that the role of the consumer had (or would very soon) change for the better.*'[39] Lev Manovich adds that the term is a tautology. According to the author of *The Language of New Media*, every content that presents itself in a digital environment is interactive by definition.[40] The same problem occurs when we attempt to define interactivity in our physical environment. The Son-O-House in Eindhoven, designed by the Dutch architect Lars Spuybroek, is a pavilion that reacts to the movements of those present. The interior of the pavilion is equipped with loudspeakers and infrared sensors. The movements of those present are registered by sensors whose every signal is linked to a specific sound effect.[41] Is there mention of interactivity here? In comparison to the workings of a climate installation or air-conditioning, the interaction between the building and those present is not so very different. Perhaps this is one of the reasons why people think that the term interactivity is often rather vacuous.

To obtain a better grasp of the concept of interactivity, we must abandon the simplest definition that describes interactivity as the ongoing interplay of the subject with its environment. This descriptive definition clarifies little more than that we are always interactive because we react to the stimuli we continually receive from the people and things around us. A different definition of interactivity would seem to be more applicable.[42] This definition claims that interactivity can breach the difference in position between the individual author and the general public. Whereas classical mass media such as radio and television force the consumer into a passive role and are the embodiment of the one-to-many role, the interactivity of digital media allows a different form of co-operation that we described as the many-to-many model. With this, we encounter a fundamental development that also touches upon the functioning of the processes of virtuality, connectivity, and multimediality.

142]

Although the model of the many-to-many is more interactive in its nature than the classical model of one-to-many, this says little about the specific form of urbanity to which this can lead. A third definition of interactivity is needed for this, a definition that not only describes the capability to intervene in a spatial stratification in an exploratory and constructive manner, but also one that refutes the alleged neutrality of interactive technologies. Isn't a game a perfect example of an exploratory and constructive form of interaction? Due to the fact that a player intervenes in the course of the game, the virtual environments in which he is situated change. We take the immediate influence that the player can exert on his environment by navigating and shooting as the exploratory component, and the capability to add new components to the game as the constructive element. These two sides – one exploratory and the other constructive – converge when we take interactivity as the possibility to link open and closed systems with one another in the physical space of the city. Interactivity can then be compared to a coupling of systems that, in the words of Gilles Deleuze, can be understood as *'a relocation of a centre of gravity on an abstract line'*. In this third definition we can locate interactivity exactly at the point where one system blends into the other. An interactive environment can be described as an open environment that connects a number of closed systems to one another. The concept of interactivity is therefore always in relation to an environment. In addition, interactivity is not a neutral or value-free entity but rather an entrance point to a different spatiality, sphere, or neighbourhood.

This last notion of interactivity not only clarifies the way in which systems mutually affect one another, it also visualizes how new systems detach themselves to function relatively independently of their context. Thus, interactivity ought to be viewed in relation to the social surroundings. This is also the political side of nodal urbanity. In this vision, architecture provides the connection that makes it possible for someone to move from one separate space to the other. We should keep in mind that offering or refusing access remains one of the most important functions of architecture. This architecture, which is responsible for the enhanced importance of information and communications processes in the monitoring of people, goods, capital, images and sounds, makes it possible to connect spaces to one another in order to function subsequently as closed systems. That is why we must remain alert: nodal urbanity can also lead to radical differentiation in the use of urban space.

We can easily chart the groups that are excluded from certain spaces: the homeless, prostitutes, prisoners, addicts. Are these people – to apply a term used by the Italian philosopher Giorgio Agamben – the new *homines sacri* of the *polis*? The phenomenon of the Urban Container is closely linked to this. Which forms of exclusion occur here? Although exclusion always takes place on the basis of the rules that are valid at that place, there are two exclusion techniques that are remarkably conspicuous. The first is based on the profiles of certain people. It is assumed that certain individuals possess specific characteristics that indicate a heightened risk of criminal behaviour. Whereas no criminal behaviour has actually taken place, the risk that it might occur is estimated as being so high that these people are refused access to the facilities of an urban space.[43]

A second form of exclusion can be distinguished, again oriented toward people or groups instead of toward the crimes committed. In contrast to the first form of exclusion, this form involves the refusal of people who have been found guilty of violating certain rules in the past. Despite this difference in gradation, the similarity between both forms of exclusion is evident. Both are directed toward the identification of 'Evil' in the form of potential threats or possible security risks in a demarcated space. Who can now claim that buildings are neutral objects when they are equipped with technologies connected to computer networks that not only enable the exclusion of people from the facilities in concrete areas but also from the social life that takes place there? Instead of an open form, there is mention of a relatively closed form of interactivity. It is against this background that we must again examine the way in which open and closed spaces in the city are related to one another. This issue embraces more than a non-obligatory articulation of architectural principles. We must study the dangers attached to nodal urbanity. In other words, which mixture of hubs do we actually wish to have in our cities?

THE ACTUALITY OF NODAL URBANITY

We should not regard architecture as the predominant means of shaping a city, of arranging it, or even of establishing it. Architecture is a link in the complex of media processes in which it has nestled. Paul Virilio anticipated this challenge when he argued that, to an ever-decreasing degree, the foundation of architecture will be physical space or a material form. He speaks of a technological time-space in which the representation of the city is no longer determined by the ceremonial entrance of the city gates or a series of streets and squares. The technological time-space of the city, which Castells describes as a hybrid of the space of flows and the space of places has a complex layering due to the fact that next to virtuality the three other processes – interactivity, connectivity, and multimediality – play a mayor role in this. Although each of these processes has a lengthy history and has developed via various media, they have reached a collective point at which they consistently reinforce one another at global level. They converge in hubs that we refer to as nodal urbanity.

144]

Nodal urbanity is not primarily oriented toward the design of high-rise apartment blocks, bridges and motorways. It cannot be found in a clear-cut or static approach to space. Instead of being finite in its definition, it is flexible and borrows its form from the context in which it is entrenched. For this reason, it cannot be over-emphasized that nodal urbanity is not a metaphor. If it were, it would be a concept to gain control of the processes that we cannot conceptualize by means of the physical structures of the city. Deleuze states: *'It is never a matter of metaphor; there are no metaphors, only combinations.'* [44] By means of nodal urbanity, we demonstrate how the urbanity of the twenty-first century can be approached with processes other than physical ones, and we can outline the corresponding transformations. The research on the phenomenon we have called the 'Urban Container', 'sonic spatiality', 'scenius' and 'sound communities' fits in with the more inclusive study of the four immanent processes of virtuality, interactivity, connectivity, and multimediality.

The physical structure and organization of the city is rooted in the medial infrastructure of these mutually reinforcing processes. But another phenomenon also occurs. Not only does urbanity become the bearer of media processes, but those same heterogeneous processes are also increasingly finding their representation in architecture. As we have seen, the immaterial processes can be described in spatial terms, but the crucial point is to determine how nodal urbanity entails the specific use and a new experience of the physical space. After all, when it involves the use of urban space, it turns out that the space is dependent on unpredictable combinations and shifts within the processes described. The primary task of architecture is to create the conditions that enable the embedding of urban space in the social or medial fabric.

[145

In concrete terms, this means that the geographical space of the city ought to be regarded as an open field or a media infrastructure that can actualize itself continually. If we wish to employ the term 'urbanity' to say something about our environment and the way in which we shape our lives and identity, we can only do so by directly involving what is actual and current in the mediascapes processes. We only need to refer to the philosophy of Deleuze: *'The virtual is fully real in so far as it is virtual.'* [45] To Deleuze, the virtual directly influences our immediate surroundings. Virtuality and actuality are two sides of the same coin. Because every actuality immediately generates new virtualities, the interaction between the mediascape processes is not a one-off occurrence. It is more of an infinite process of generation. In philosophical terms: in the determining of place of the *polis*, the actualization of the nodal hubs indicates a process of repeatedly new and changing articulations of urbanity.

Isn't this one of the reasons why urbanity consistently assumes a different form within various contexts? In the immediate relationship between the present and the mediascape processes – the actual and the world-embracing – the flows find their path due to the force of the nodal hubs, while they, in turn, depend on the working of the varying mediascape processes. We can describe those hubs in urban terms because concrete social environments and spaces converge, sample, multiply, or exchange positions there. The population migrations in Afrofuturism, the intermedial space of Urban youth culture, and the large-scale environments of MMORPGs such as *World of Warcraft* are only a few examples. The consequences of this development differ strongly according to place and time. Depending on the force of these processes, these nodal hubs will also have an effect in physical space, will become larger, expand, shrink, or even vanish altogether. That is the reason why we do not regard urbanity as a passive wrapping but rather as a continual process of materialization and dematerialization of virtuality, multimediality, connectivity and interactivity.

AWAY FROM EVERY FUTURE

146]

Does the challenge of nodal architecture mean that we must aim to turn closed systems into open networks? Although these processes may construct complex spatialities and establish operational connections, it is nevertheless the case that, if we emphasize only this aspect, the way in which we experience this same environment remains underexposed. Henri Lefebvre's studies of everyday urban space and Michel Foucault's analysis of the Panopticon of Jeremy Bentham show that spatiality is primarily a social phenomenon. In other words, architecture is nothing more than the relationships it enters into with people, animals or objects. What has received little attention until now is the fact that a different (self-)consciousness also arises among the residents or those present in a nodal urbanity. Even more influential than the effects of the four media processes on the (de-)materialized form of the city is probably the fact that a change in our self-perception occurs along with the forming of nodal urbanity. We refer to this self-perception as 'post-paranoia'.

Without wishing to lapse into a play of cause and effect, the question must be posed one more time. Who emerges unscathed from the mediascape of popular culture? Let us take the *Hikikomori* as an example of a generation of screenagers whose lives are completely devoted to new media such as internet and video games. What happens to a young person when he has been shut away in the multiverse of games for years? Does he react differently to the stimuli that his body receives from the physical environment of the city? Do his brains furnish him with impulses to react more quickly to the events that happen all around him? Every medium articulates our experience in a different way. Painting offers the viewers a different experience of space and time than what the gamer receives in his navigation through the virtual world of a computer game. The webcam constructs a different notion of time-space than television does. This illustrates one of the most important effects of nodal urbanity. Not only the urban space has changed but there is also a gradual change in our own experience of the world and ourselves. The cause of this change is not really based on the physical definition of the urban space, or the floor plans of buildings, or the situation of squares and streets. It is rather the effect of virtual, interactive, connective and multimedia processes that influence our attitude and our self-awareness. This does not mean that these processes are the only, or even the most determining, factors in the transformation of our consciousness; other developments such as ethnographic, financial and political changes also play a role. However, this does not make the significance of these processes with the scapes or flows less important.[46]

[147

The observation that immaterial physics have visible effects on our physical bodies and self-awareness leads to two conclusions. The enormous influence of popular culture ensures that we adopt new skills. An excellent example of this is the proliferation of the video game. In the era of interactive media, the gamer is the symbol for a new type of user who no longer resembles the television viewer lazing in his armchair, passively perceiving image and sound. On the contrary, a gamer is a bundle of concentration and alertness. He is a master of the game right down to his fingertips. Zapping and clicking, he moves the mouse or scroller through the virtual environments that unfold before his eyes. We are witness to the transition from a *lean backward* to a *lean forward* medium. Whereas a lean backward medium such as film or television presupposes a passive attitude of the viewer, a lean forward medium requires an active attitude. The player leans forward and navigates with the greatest possible attention through virtual environments that he can alter with a single action.

In addition to the fact that the above-described processes lead to new skills, the processes also influence our self-awareness. Until now, this kind of influence was always reserved for traditional forms of architecture, such as schools, hospitals and prisons. Bentham's eighteenth-century Panopticon is an excellent example of the last-mentioned. The round shape with a tower in the middle from which the guards could view the cells on the inside of the ring was sufficient to impose coercive behavioural codes on the residents, with the aim of cultivating a positive identity. Architecture not only influences the consciousness of the users here, but also determines it to a large extent. To find this kind of influence in nodal urbanity, we must shift our attention to the four immaterial processes of the mediascapes. To which intensification of our self-perception does this complex of media processes lead?

Nowadays, we recoil less and less from giving technology a place in our daily lives. It seems as if the anxiety for all forms of technology last appeared in the seventies of the previous century. This was prominently expressed in the work of William Burroughs, who repeatedly warned us of the invisible and all-penetrating effects of technology [47] In *The Naked Lunch*, dating from 1959, he wrote: '*The logical extension of encephalographic research is biocontrol; that is control of physical movement, mental processes, emotional reactions and apparent sensory impressions by means of bioelectric signals injected into the nervous system of the subject.*' To escape this permanent monitoring, Burroughs argues in *Cities of the Red Night* in favour of the establishment of pirate republics where everyone can do what he wants. Under the leadership of Captain Mission, free communities ought to be founded in which complete equality prevails. In the last few years before his death, Burroughs placed all his hope in outer space. He believed that only outer space offered an opportunity of escaping the forms of control that accompany far-reaching influence of new technologies on our daily living environment.

148]

It requires little argument that present-day technological processes do not guarantee that our lives will become much better or much worse. The distrust of technology is gradually disappearing because it has become an integral part of our lives. Accordingly, in his *Regeln für den Menschenpark*, Peter Sloterdijk speaks of a new era in which we not only approach our direct environment differently, but in which history and the future have been allocated a different position. We no longer seek reference in history or in the future in order to find security. From the point of view of nodal urbanity, we must draw the logical conclusion that we no longer have any kind of future. The future is embedded in the actualization of the mediascape processes: virtuality, interactivity, connectivity and multimediality. It is thus already immediately present. William Gibson articulates this splendidly: '*The future is here. It's just not widely distributed yet'*. The fact that the future no longer lies before us does not mean that every form of paranoia has vanished. Burroughs is still abundantly represented among us. We should not be disappointed at this. This means that we are witness to a different relationship with the embedding of media technologies and processes. No longer interested in the past or the future, the origin of things or the end of affairs, we only orient our attention to the continual actualization of nodal hubs or specific forms of urbanity.

[149

Postscript

Pick up any newspaper and you will see that the city is synonymous [151 with problems. Crime, smog, traffic jams, segregation, and social deprivation colour our picture of the city. Although it is certainly not a paradise on Earth, the city is nevertheless the most favoured topic of pop culture. From *Vice City* in the *Grand Theft Auto* game to the beats of *Techno City*, the city's power of attraction on pop culture is not diminished by the prevailing problems. In contrast, they are regarded as a major challenge. In the game entitled *SimCity*, which focuses on designing and running a city, much attention is devoted to the prevention of crime, nuisance, and pollution. In *SimCity 4*, population groups that are hostile to one another even have to be kept apart.

Although many authors have discussed the enormous influence of pop culture upon our living environment, no comprehensive study investigating the relationship between the city and pop culture has yet taken place, as far as we know. We regard *Mediapolis* as a first step in that direction. The book offers a bird's-eye view of the nature of urban pop culture and the role it plays in our concept of the city. This is not a clear, unambiguous relationship. The liaison between pop culture and the city is too stratified for that. The complex relationship between them is echoed in the slogan of *SimCity*: 'Be God, Be Mayor ... Be You'. The slogan expresses the fact that we are always in a correlation with the *planet* we live on, the *community* we are part of, and our physical *body*. It is not only a pastime; pop culture's enormous influence on these three entities gives it unprecedented power.

Be God. When we orient our attention to the first angle of approach, the extent to which the *planet* is caught up in the ruthless march toward globalization becomes evident. It is common to approach globalization from the standpoint of worldwide flows of capital, goods and information, driven by new communications technologies. But the Earth is also surrounded by the culture of the popular media. Games such as *America's Army, World of Warcraft* and *Grand Theft Auto* and the music of Snoop 'Doggy' Dogg, Dizzee Rascal and Juan Atkins intensify the drive toward globalization. Place, distance, and territory have become flexible concepts in those virtual and sonic environments. People from every continent meet one another in the shared environments of games and music. The images and sounds of pop culture make the Earth smaller, compacter, and more manageable than ever before. Due to the immediate impact of those same images and sounds, young people in the streets of Tokio have more affinity with the youth in Miami than with their parents or neighbours. With pop media we shape our own worlds.

152]

Be Mayor. As a result of electronic globalization, the geographic borders or territorial specifications of a country are losing their significance. Feelings of alienation and disorientation are the consequence. The disappearance of old certainties gives added importance to the issue of how *communities* are formed. The all-inclusive inner world of the Urban Container gives shape to the yearning for safety and security, but pop culture forces us to look for a notion of community in other directions as well. Electronic globalization itself possesses a spatial dimension. In the shared spatialities of games and music, we are part of a community that is no longer determined by traditional bonds and coercive factors such as national borders, origins, or race. A flexible social structure, in which specific stories, symbols and knowledge are shared and an own language created, is forming around expressions of pop culture. These self-created communities are mostly based on a shared interest in certain games or music styles. Although these social convergences have a thin form and the relationships in these new environments are unstable and ephemeral, they do guarantee secure and sheltered accommodation at least temporarily.

Be You. Pop culture makes its mark on our everyday living environment. What sounds like an innocent pop number or seems to comprise little more than a simple shooting game on internet is actually part of an experience that is shared by millions of people all over the world. While pop culture not only has a direct influence at this global level and at the level of communities linked by the media, the impulses of the synthetic pop world are also making an increasingly strong physical impact. Popular culture establishes a direct relationship with our *body*. It uses the mass media to bombard our senses with seductive images, rhythms, and sounds. A rhythm sets our body in motion, whether we want to our not. At our weakest moments, we are little more than zombies whose natural urges are activated. For a long time people thought that pop culture leads to passivity: while spread out on sofas or in armchairs we allowed the world to come to us via the screen and loudspeakers. As pop culture further invaded daily life, our anatomy evolved with it. The spinal curvature of the certified couch potato has altered. We are now bent over keyboards, gamepads, and turntables. This physical change is coupled to a modified attitude toward the media. In the meantime, the media have become fully integrated in the information and communication technologies of electronic globalization and they form the core of our thought and action. Accordingly, we now speak of an experience of post-paranoia.

Every generation builds its own cities. Now that these cities have uprooted themselves from their foundations, the concept of urbanity is losing its clearness. The city is no longer the city. For this reason, a world that is occupied by the images and sounds of popular culture requires a new theory of urbanity. This theory must relate to the aspects of virtuality, multimediality, interactivity, and connectivity.

[153

Introduction

1. M. Berman, *All That Is Solid Melts into Air: The Experience of Modernity*, New York, Penguin Books, 1988, p. 290.

2. A. Appadurai, *Modernity at Large. Cultural Dimensions of Globalization*, Minneapolis, The University of Minnesota Press, 1996, p. 35.

3. For a topical overview of the number of paying users of Massively Multiplayer Online Games, see the following site: **www.mmogchart.com**. Date of visit: 15 June 2006.

4. V. Mosco, *The Digital Sublime. Myth, Power, and Cyberspace*, Cambridge/Massachusetts, The MIT Press, 2004

5. 'Sim Civics', in: *The Boston Globe*, 7 August 2005, **www.boston.com/news/globe/ideas/articles/2005/08/07/sim_civics/**. Date of visit: 28 February 2006.

Part One: Virtual Urbanity

Chapter 1: The Militarization of Life

1. *'Empower yourself, defend freedom'* was the slogan of the *America's Army* game during the E3 game conference in Los Angeles, 2004.

2. For a further elaboration of the military entertainment complex, see the following articles: D. Nieborg, 'Militaire Game(r)s: Vechten in de Virtuele Werkelijkheid', in: *Tijdschrift voor Mediageschiedenis*, Amsterdam, Boom, 2004; T. Lenoir and H. Lowood, 'Theaters of War: The Military-Entertainment Complex' (2002), **www.stanford.edu/class/sts145/Library/Lenoir-Lowood_Theaters OfWar.pdf**. Date of visit: 18 November 2005.

3. S. Žižek, *Het subject en zijn onbehagen. Vijf essays over psychoanalyse en het cartesiaanse cogito*, Amsterdam, Boom, 1997, p. 149.

4. D. Becker, 'Army gunning for game players' (2004), **http://news.zdnet.com/2100-3513_22-5211682.html**. Date of visit: 18 November 2005.

5. G. De Meyer, 'De kritiek op videogames, met name inzake geweld', **www.kuleuven.ac.be/videogames/pop/pagina7.html**. Date of visit: 18 November 2005.

6. Atari Battlezone, **http://markn.users.netlink.co.uk/Arcade/battz.html**. Date of visit: 18 November 2005.

7. R. Riddell, 'Doom Goes To War' (1997), **www.wired.com/wired/archive/5.04/ff_doom_pr.html**. Date of visit: 18 November 2005.

8. From the beginning of the twentieth century onward, pictures of bombardments, victims, and soldiers have not been discarded but recycled in feature films. See: P. Virilio, *The Vision Machine*, Bloomington, Indiana University Press, 1995, p. 50.

9. C. Clover, 'Natural-born killers will not win hearts and minds' (2004), **www.christusrex.org/www1/news/ft-6-x27-04.html**. Date of visit: 18 November 2005.

10. C. Clover, 'Natural-born killers will not win hearts and minds', o.c.

11. 'Interview: Pandemic Full Spectrum Warrior' (2003), **www.xboxaddict. com/interviews/view_interview.php?Interview_ID=40**. Date of visit: 18 November 2005.

12. 'Oral History: The Commanders', **www.pbs.org/wgbh/pages/frontline/ gulf/oral/commanders.html**. Date of visit: 18 November 2005.

13. D. Becker, 'Army gunning for game players' (2004), o.c.

14. M. Foucault, *Surveiller et Punir. Naissance de la prison* (Discipline and Punish. The Birth of the Prison), Paris, Gallimard, 1975, p. 57.

15. G. Deleuze, *Pourparlers. 1972–1990* (Negotiations. 1972–1990), Paris, Minuit, 1990, pp. 240–247.

16. D. Garland, *The Culture of Control. Crime and Social Order in Contemporary Society*, Oxford, Oxford University Press, 2001.

17. D. Garland, *The Culture of Control*, o.c., p. 11.

18. J. Sonauer, 'Preview and Interview: America's Army' (2002), **www.simhq. com/simhq3/sims/interviews/americasarmy/index.shtml**. Date of visit: 18 November 2005.

19. Interview with the Dutch Minister for Health, Hans Hoogervorst, in *de Volkskrant* daily newspaper, 15 April 2005.

20. M. Davis, *Ecology of Fear. Los Angeles and the Imagination of Disaster*, New York, Vintage Books, 1999, p. 366. The analysis of Mike Davis has led to much criticism, especially his Marxist interpretation of the social polarization in Los Angeles. K.J. Hayward, *City Limits: Crime, Consumer Culture and the Urban Experience*, London, The Glass House, 2004, pp. 114–145.

21. We see this change of perspective in *America's Army*. In *America's Army* all the players are Americans; each player has the American nationality. For that reason, it makes no difference whatsoever if a player actually lives in Belgium or North Korea, he is always placed in an American unit. This means that it is impossible to fight against American soldiers. The opponent sees the other player as an enemy of the USA and himself as a *US trooper*. This way this works is shown by one of the missions in which a team of players have to liberate American prisoners of war from a terrorist camp. During this mission, the opposing party has to prevent their prisoners being freed from the American camp by terrorists.

Chapter 2: The Architecture of the Urban Container

22. 'Oral History of Bertrand Goldberg', interviewed by Betty J. Blum, Chicago, The Art Institute of Chicago, 1992, p. 154, **www.artic.edu/aic/libraries/ caohp/goldberg.pdf**. Date of visit: 9 January 2006.

23. 'Oral History of Bertrand Goldberg', o.c., p. 170.

[155

24. A. Wogenscky, The Unité d'Habitation at Marseille, in: *Le Corbusier: The Garland Essays* (Allen Brooks, H., ed.), New York, Garland Publishing, 1987, p. 117.

25. At present, advertisements are being made for a gigantic (cruise) ship, a floating Urban Container, for a new form of co-habitation. *'The ship is as large as it is, simply because that is the minimum size required to make the community economically self-sustaining and a desirable and attractive place to live.'* See: **www.freedomship.com**. Date of visit: 15 February 2006.

26. Although most company towns were founded between 1830 and 1930, the term 'company town' only came into general use at the end of the nineteenth century, when it was applied to mining settlements in the United States. The company town differed from the industrial city and the corporation town in that everything was owned by one company. See: J.S. Garner (ed.), *The Company Town, Architecture and Society in the Early Industrial Age*, Oxford, Oxford University Press, 1992.

156]

27. In the eighteenth century, the encapsulation of public areas by enterprises also took place in Europe. The most striking example is the settlement around the salt refineries at Chaux by the architect Claude-Nicolas Ledoux (1736–1806). In the French district of Arc-et-Senans, Ledoux designed an architectural configuration in the form of a semi-circle with a diameter of 370 metres. The technical installations and the houses of the workers were placed within this building complex. Because the design did not have the intention to separate the various facets of life, architects like Le Corbusier regarded the salt refinery as an expression of the ideal society. Production did not remain invisible, but was an integrated component of the company town. The encapsulation of the various social functions is indicated by the remark made by Ledoux that he wished to create a complex *'that brings together all the kinds of buildings used in the social order.'*

28. G. Deleuze, *Pourparlers*, o.c., pp. 240–247.

Chapter 3: The Bankruptcy of the Street

29. H. Arendt, *The Human Condition*, Chicago, The University of Chicago Press, 1958, p. 57.

30. V. Grassmuck, 'I'm alone, but not lonely' (1990), **www.cjas.org/~leng/otaku-e.htm**. Date of visit: 10 March 2006.

31. W. Gibson, 'Modern boys and mobile girls', in: *The Observer*, 1 April 2001, **http://observer.guardian.co.uk/life/story/0,6903,466391,00.html**. Date of visit: 9 January 2006.

32. R. Murakami, 'Japan's Lost Generation', in: *Time Magazine*, 1 May 2000, **www.time.com/time/asia/magazine/2000/0501/japan.essaymurakami.html**. Date

of visit: 9 January 2006.

33. R. Murakami, 'Japan's Lost Generation', o.c.

34. M. Foucault, *Histoire de la sexualité 1– La volonté de savoir* (The Will to Knowledge), Paris, Gallimard, 1976, p. 125.

35. H. Bey, *T.A.Z. The Temporary Autonomous Zone, Ontological Anarchy, Poetic Terrorism*, New York, Autonomedia, 1991, p. 101.

36. N. Klein, *No Logo*, Flamingo, London, 2000, p. 320.

37. N. Klein, 'Reclaiming the Commons', in: *New Left Review* 9, May–June 2001, p. 82, **www.newleftreview.com/NLR24305.shtml**. Date of visit: 9 January 2006.

38. An extraordinary variant of Culture Jamming is performed by a collective that calls itself 'The Yes Men' (**www.theyesmen.org**). The Yes Men orient their endeavours to the domain of the internet. They copied the website of the World Trade Organization under the name of its precursor GATT (**www.gatt.org**). People who wish to come in contact with the WTO thus land at the simulated site of The Yes Men. Eventually, The Yes Men were even invited to speak at conferences on behalf of the WTO. A report is made of these activities in the documentary of the same name.

39. Mommaas, H. (i.c. Knulst, W. and Van den Heuvel, M.), *De vrijetijdsindustrie in stad en land, een studie naar de markt van belevenissen, WRR Voorstudies en achtergronden*, The Hague, SDU Uitgevers, 2000, p. 85.

40. In *Vertoog over verzet. Politiek in tijden van globalisering*, Dieter Lesage researches the possibility of resistance in the capitalist liberal democracy. He uses the term 'Empire' from the philosophers Hardt and Negri to refer to the working of this capitalist democracy. In his book, he announces the upsurge of a new class: the digitariat. This is the class that has nothing but a computer and an internet connection: translators, programmers, web designers, text writers, and editors.

41. J. de Mul, *Cyberspace Odyssee*, Kampen, Klement, 2003, p. 180.

42. M. Castells, *The Information Age: Economy, Society and Culture. The Rise of the Network Society, Volume I*, Oxford, Blackwell Publishers Ltd, 1996, p. 403; M. Castells, *The Information Age: Economy, Society and Culture. End of Millennium, Volume III*, Oxford, Blackwell Publishers Ltd, 1998, p. 253.

43. Anne-Marie Schleiner, interviewed by Pedro Soler for SonarOnline: **www.opensorcery.net/interviewp.html**. Date of visit: 9 January 2006. Despite the negative reactions to the game, one thing has become clear. *Velvet-Strike* offers resistance within the rules or protocols of the existing game of *Counterstrike*. *Velvet-Strike* assumes the shape of the *Counterstrike* game in order to effectively influence the underlying network.

44. M. Foucault, *Histoire de la sexualité 1– La volonté de savoir*, o.c., p. 126.

[157

45. News Tribune, 'Hezbollah computer game takes propaganda war on Israel to virtual battlefield' (2004), **www.newstribune.com/articles/2003/05/25/ex port16774.txt**. Date of visit: 11 January 2006.

46. M. Foucault, 'L'éthique du souci de soi comme practique de la liberté', in: *Dits et écrits*, Paris, Gallimard, 1994.

47. 'Under Ash, Arabs' first video game' (2002), **www.middle-east-online. com/english/Default.pl?id=317=317&format=0**. Date of visit: 11 January 2006.

48. News Tribune, 'Hezbollah computer game takes propaganda war on Israel to virtual battlefield' (2004), o.c., Date of visit: 11 January 2006.

49. D.J. Wakin, 'Video Game Mounts Simulated Attacks Against Israeli Targets' (2003), **www.nytimes.com/2003/05/18/international/middleeast/18VIDE. html?ex=1368590400&en=d04c67f3901c3721&ei=5007&partner=USERLAND**. Date of visit: 11 January 2006.

50. M. Foucault, 'What is Enlightenment?', in: P. Rabinow (ed.), *The Foucault Reader*, London, Penguin, 1984, pp. 32–50.

51. Here, one is not speaking of an Arabian subject in the sense of a lifestyle or existential aesthetics in the significance that Foucault assigns in the last two volumes of *Histoire de la sexualité* (The History of Sexuality). He regards this as the capability to turn a life into a work of art that survives his fleeting existence. Life is thus forced into a ritual and a style. Nineteenth-century dandyism, personified by Oscar Wilde, is an excellent example of this.

Part Two: Sonic Urbanity

Chapter 1: The Audio-Hallucinatory Spheres of the City

1. In 1927, 'Bucky' Fuller conceived the *Dymaxion House*: a hexagonal metal cell that is suspended on a central vertical axis like a bicycle wheel. The house can be built in a factory, just like a car, and can be installed anywhere.

2. P. Cook, *Archigram*, London, Studio Vista Publishers, 1972.

3. W. Asbeek Brusse, H. van Dalen, B. Wissink, *Stad en land in een nieuwe geografie. Maatschappelijke veranderingen en ruimtelijke dynamiek*, Wetenschappelijke Raad voor het Regeringsbeleid (WRR), The Hague, SDU Uitgevers, 2002, p. 89.

4. See also: M. Cobussen, 'Verkenningen van/in een muzikale ruimte. Over Peter Sloterdijk en Edwin van der Heide', in: *Interakta #5, Grootstedelijke reflecties. Over kunst en openbare ruimte* (H.A.F. Oosterling and S. Thissen, ed.), Rotterdam, Faculty of Philosophy at Erasmus University Rotterdam, 2002.

5. A. Toffler, *The Third Wave* (1980), New York, Bantam Books, 1990, p. 150.

6. S. Reynolds, *Energy Flash. A Journey Through Rave Music and Dance Cul-*

ture, London, Picador, 1998, p. 9.

7. P. Sloterdijk, *Mediatijd* (translation of: *Der starke Grund, zusammen zu sein. Erinnerungen an die Erfindung des Volkes*, Frankfurt am Main, Suhrkamp, 1998, and: *Medien-Zeit. Drei Gegenwartsdiagnostische Versuche*, Stuttgart, Cantz, 1993), Amsterdam, Boom, 1999, p. 94.

8. P. Sloterdijk, *Spären III. Schäume*, Frankfurt am Main, Suhrkamp, 2004, p. 379.

9. P. Sloterdijk, *Mediatijd*, o.c., p. 94.

10. See also: S. Thissen, 'Wat is 'Urban Culture'? (My Adidas)', 2004/2005, **www.siebethissen.net**. Date of visit: 17 March 2006.

11. Besides 'urbanus', Urban is also linked to the word 'urbs' meaning 'large city'. 'Urbs' has the same origins as the word 'orbis' which refers to a ring or circle. In that sense 'urbs' is a large city that is surrounded by walls.

12. A. Ogg, *The Men Behind Def Jam. The Radical Rise of Russell Simmons and Rick Rubin*, London, Omnibus Press, 2002, p. 4.

13. A. Ogg, *The Men Behind Def Jam*, o.c., p. 19.

14. A. Rossi, *The Architecture of the City*, Cambridge/Massachusetts, The MIT Press, 1999, p. 112.

Chapter 2: Sampladelic Spatialities

15. D. Diederichsen, 'Es streamt so sexy. Die Dialektiek von Clicks & Cuts', in: *Popvisionen. Links in die Zukunft* (K. Neumann-Braun, A. Schmidt and M. Mai, ed.), Frankfurt am Main, Suhrkamp, 2003, p. 60.

16. F. Kittler, *Gramophone, Film, Typewriter*, Stanford, Stanford University Press, 1999, p. 27.

17. See: B. Eno, 'The Studio as Compositional Tool', in: *Audio Culture. Readings in Modern Music* (C. Cox and D. Warner, ed.), New York, The Continuum International Publishing Group Inc, 2002, p. 127.

18. Music is a central theme in the thinking of Pythagoras. By linking his interest in music to mathematics, he laid the basis for modern mathematics. In this way he managed to enter the realm of astronomy, conceived the theory of mathematical *sphaerai*, and the theory of ethereal music and that of the harmony of the spheres. From Pythagoras to the Middle Ages, music was thus connected to mathematics. See: Iannis Xenakis, *The Man and His Music: A Conversation With the Composer and a Description of His Works*, Westport, Greenwood Press, 1967, p. 14.

19. H. Russcol, *The Liberation of Sound: An Introduction to Electronic Music*, Englewood Cliffs, Prentice-Hall, 1972, p. 32.

20. W. Benjamin, 'The Work of Art in the Age of Mechanical Reproduction'

(1936), in: *Illuminations*, London, Pimlico, 1999, p. 218.

21. M. Dery, Black to the Future: Afro-futurism 1.0, **www.levity.com/mard ery/black.html**. Date of visit: 20 March 2006.

22. See also the internet sites **www.afrofuturism.com** and **http://groups.yahoo. com/group/afrofuturism**. Within the theory-forming on Afrofuturism, writers and artists exchange ideas on ethnicity and culture in relation to technology. In this way, a counterweight is offered to ideas of internet as an infinite space in which gender and race play no role whatsoever. Although many diverse topics are discussed in Afrofuturism – album covers, posters, party flyers, and the outfits of artists are only a few examples – we approach it from a sonic perspective. In doing so, we follow Mark Dery who links black futurism to the sonic range in order to refute fixed images of the future.

23. P.D. Miller, Algorithms. Erasures and the Art of Memory, in: *Audio Culture*, o.c., p. xiv.

24. S. Hall, 'What Is This "Black" in Black Popular Culture?', in: *Black Popular Culture* (G. Dent, ed.), Seattle, Bay Press, 1992, pp. 21–23.

25. S. Reynolds, *Energy Flash*, o.c., p. 366.

26. S. Reynolds, *Energy Flash*, o.c., pp. 364–365.

27. See: K. Eshun, *More Brilliant Than the Sun. Adventures in Sonic Fiction*, London, Quartet Books, 1998.

28. G. Delanty, *Community*, London/New York, Routledge, 2003, pp. 179–180.

29. P. Sloterdijk, *Sphären III. Schäume*, o.c., p. 57.

30. A. Nelson, Introduction: Future Texts, in: *Social Text*, no. 71, Durham, Duke University Press, 2002, p. 7.

31. Steve Goodman, interviewed by Alex de Jong and Marc Schuilenburg: **www.studiopopcorn.com/01-artikelen/interviews/goodman.html**. Date of visit: 20 March 2006.

32. G. Deleuze and F. Guattari, *Mille plateaux. Capitalisme et schizophrénie 2* (A Thousands Plateaux. Capitalism and Schizophrenia), Paris, Minuit, 1980, p. 430.

Part Three: Nodal Urbanity
Chapter 1: From Genius to Scenius

1. T. Baumeister, *De filosofie en de kunsten, Van Plato tot Beuys*, Nijmegen, Damon, 1999, p. 166.

2. A. van den Braembussche, *Denken over kunst, Een inleiding in de kunstfilosofie*, Bussum, Coutinho, 2000, p. 165.

3. A. van den Braembussche, *Denken over kunst*, o.c., p. 165.

4. P. Deamer, 'Branding the Architectural Author', in: Perspecta 37, 'Famous', Cambridge/London, MIT Press, 2005, p. 44.

5. B. Eno, *A Year With Swollen Appendices: The Diary of Brian Eno*, London, Faber and Faber ltd, 1996, pp. 354–355.

6. D. Becker, 'Game publishers sweat console change', **http://news.com.com/ Game+publishers+sweat+console+change/2100-1043_3-5377871.html**. Date of visit: 3 December 2005.

7. S.L. Kent, *The Ultimate History of Video Games. From Pong to Pokémon and Beyond–The Story Behind the Craze That Touched Our Lives and Changed The World*, New York, Prima Publishing, 2001, p. 459.

8. See also: Edge Magazine, 'The Modern Age', The Mod Scene: What Happens When Gamers Build Games?, Bath, Future Publishing Ltd., 2003, no. 126.

9. 'Can you trust Wikipedia?', in: *The Guardian*, 24 October 2005, **http:// technology.guardian.co.uk/opinion/story/0,16541,1599325,00.html**. Date of visit: 23 January 2006.

10. H. Jenkins, *Textual Poachers. Television Fans and Participatory Culture*, New York, Routledge, 1992, p. 13.

11. H. Jenkins, *Textual Poachers*, o.c., p. 10.

12. H. Jenkins, *Textual Poachers*, o.c., p. 18.

13. M. Hardt and A. Negri, *Multitude. War and Democracy In The Age Of Empire*, New York, Penguin Press, 2004, p. 338.

14. E.S. Raymond, *The Cathedral and the Bazaar* (2000), **www.catb.org/~esr/ writings/cathedral-bazaar/cathedral-bazaar**. Date of visit: 28 February 2006.

15. M. Provoost, B. Colenbrander, F. Alkemade, *Dutchtown. O.M.A.'s meesterproef in Almere*, Rotterdam, NAi publishers, 1999, p. 82.

16. The American researcher Mark Granovetter has discovered that more than half of the people in the USA find a job due to an acquaintance, but that more than 80% of these people scarcely know who their helper is. Granovetter concluded that it is not who you know well that is important but rather who you don't know well. He refers to this as the power of weak links. Only the weak links introduce new knowledge into a network. As a result, the network receives new impulses and the opportunity to renew itself.

17. C. Weeber, *Het wilde wonen*, Rotterdam, 010 Publishers, 1998.

[161

Chapter 2: The City in a Flooded World

18. A. Appadurai, *Modernity at Large. Cultural Dimensions of Globalization*, Minneapolis, The University of Minnesota Press, 1996, p. 31.

19. In their work *Splintering Urbanism* Stephen Graham and Simon Marvin display how infrastructural changes influence cities and urbanity. In their opin-

ion, to gain a good understanding of the city one should look at the effects of technological infrastructures that realize new connections at local and regional levels. See: S. Graham and S. Marvin, *Splintering Urbanism. Networked Infrastructures, Technological Mobilities and the Urban Condition*, London, Routledge, 2001.

20. M. Castells, *The Information Age: Economy, Society and Culture. The Rise of the Network Society*, Volume I, Oxford, Blackwell Publishers Ltd, 1996, p. 442.

21. W. Gibson, *Neuromancer*, London, HarperCollinsPublishers, 1993, p. 67.

22. J.P. Barlow, *Cyberspace Declaration of Independence*, Davos, Switzerland, 8 February 1996, **www.homes.eff.org/~barlow/Declaration-Final.html**. Date of visit: 28 February 2006.

23. M. McLuhan, *The Gutenberg Galaxy. The Making of Typographic Man*, London, Routledge & Kegan Paul, 1967, p. 31.

24. 'Information' and 'communications' systems are often mentioned indiscriminately. According to the German media theorist Friedrich Kittler, however, a distinction ought to be made between these systems. Whereas information systems are oriented toward the storage, processing and sending of messages, communications systems also control the traffic in goods. The latter systems also contain all kinds of media.

25. W.J. Mitchell, *City of Bits. Space, Place, and the Infobahn*, Cambridge/Massachusetts, The MIT Press, 1995, p. 104.

26. W.J. Mitchell, *City of Bits*, o.c., p. 65.

27. W.J. Mitchell, *City of Bits*, o.c., p. 105.

28. M. Castells, *The Information Age: Economy, Society and Culture. The Rise of the Network Society*, o.c., p. 428.

29. M.C. Boyer, *CyberCities: Visual Perception in the Age of Electronic Communication*, New York, Princeton Architectural Press, 1996, p. 14.

30. M.C. Boyer, Op de grens tussen steden en CyberCities, **www.dma.be/cvb/as/kino3/DFBOYER.htm**. Date of visit: 28 February 2006.

31. M.C. Boyer, Op de grens tussen steden en CyberCities, o.c.

32. M.C. Boyer, Op de grens tussen steden en CyberCities, o.c.

33. S. Sassen, *Globalisering. Over mobiliteit van geld, mensen en informatie*, Amsterdam, Van Gennep, 1999, p. 130.

34. M. Levander, 'Where Does Fantasy End?', in: *Time Magazine*, 2001, vol. 157, no. 22.

35. M.C. Boyer, *CyberCities*, o.c., p. 150.

36. Besides games, other media have also begun to remediate other media. For example, the electronic literature of the hypertext uses images and sound to add

various layers of significance to the text. The reader becomes an active participant by clicking on links so that the story can take an unexpected turn.

37. S. Thissen, 'Logboek van de bekladde stad. De stad als massamedium', in: *EasyCity. Interventies in een verscheurde stad*, (F. Kallenberg, ed.), Amsterdam, De Vrije Ruimte, 2004.

38. G. Delanty, *Community*, London/New York, Routledge, 2003, p. 171.

39. E.J. Aarseth, *Cybertext: Perspectives on Ergodic Literature*, London, The Johns Hopkins University Press, 1997, p. 48.

40. L. Manovich, *The Language of New Media*, Cambridge/Massachusetts, The MIT Press, 2002, p. 55.

41. In the image culture of the video clip and film we see how the interaction between the user and the medium is shaped. In the clips *Love At First Sight* and *Can't Get You Out Of My Head* of the Australian singer Kylie Minogue, the buildings react to the dancing movements of the singer by changing colour to the rhythm of the music. Digital turbulence is thus caused in which it is no longer the aim to present reality by means of special effects, but rather to allow filmed reality to dissolve in the digital technology of the music. In Washington D.C. from the film *Minority Report* (2002) iris scans are used to enable hologram adverts to confront passers-by with the products they currently need. The adverts address the main character personally: *'John Anderton, we have the ideal vacation for you!'* and *'John Anderton, wouldn't you like a pint of Guinness?'*

[163

42. To offer the perspective of interactivity a wider stratification, Robert Pfaller and Slavoj Žižek discuss a different interpretation. To them, interpassivity is the sinister supplement or mirror image of interactivity. This reverse side to interactivity refers to the phenomenon that we are active by remaining passive. We are active via another person or medium. Žižek uses the example of the video recorder to demonstrate that this piece of equipment not only relieves us of the duty to look at the films that are shown every day on television, but also that we have allocated our subjectivity to another medium. If we have tapes of films in our home, we then have the idea that we can view films at any moment of the day.

43. Because they are seen as potential hijackers, it is not possible for certain individuals to fly. Another example is the exclusion of groups of young people from shopping malls on the basis of their alternative clothing style (skateboarders, gothics, etc.). See: A. Von Hirsch and C. Shearing, 'Exclusion from Public Space', in: *Ethical and Social Perspectives on Situational Crime Prevention*, Oxford, Hart Publishing, 2000.

44. G. Deleuze and C. Parnet, *Dialoques* (Dialogues), Paris, Flammarion, 1977, p. 140.

45. G. Deleuze, *Différence et répétition* (Difference and Repetition), Paris, Presses Universitaires de France, 1968, p. 269.

46. See also: J. de Mul, *Cyberspace Odyssee*, Kampen, Uitgeverij Klement, 2002, p. 192.

47. The ideas of Burroughs were later championed by philosophers such as Gilles Deleuze who, in his article *Post-scriptum sur les sociétés de contrôle* (Postscript on the Societies of Control), establishes that everything and everyone are linked by means of technological processes: *'"Control" is the name Burroughs proposes as a term for the new monster, one that Foucault recognizes as our immediate future. Paul Virilio also is continually analyzing the ultrarapid forms of free-floating control that replaced the old disciplines operating in the time frame of a closed system.'* See: G. Deleuze, *Pourparlers. 1972–1990* (Negotiations. 1972–1990), Paris, Minuit, 1990, pp. 240–247.

Aarseth, E.J., *Cybertext: Perspectives on Ergodic Literature*, London, The Johns Hopkins University Press, 1997

Agamben, G., *Homo Sacer. Sovereign Power and Bare Life*, Standford, Standford University Press, 1998

Agamben, G., *Means Without End. Notes on Politics*, Minneapolis, The University of Minneapolis Press, 2000

Agamben, G., *The Coming Community*, Minneapolis, The University of Minnesota Press, 2003

Agamben, G., *State of Exception*, Chicago, The University of Chicago Press, 2005

Appadurai, A., *Modernity at Large. Cultural Dimensions of Globalization*, Minneapolis, The University of Minnesota Press, 1996

Arendt, H., *The Human Condition*, Chicago, The University of Chicago Press, 1958

Asbeek Brusse, W., Dalen, van H., Wissink, B., *Stad en land in een nieuwe geografie. Maatschappelijke veranderingen en ruimtelijke dynamiek*, Wetenschappelijke Raad voor het Regeringsbeleid (WRR), Den Haag, Sdu Uitgevers, 2002

Badiou, A., *L'Être et l'Événement* (Being and Event), Paris, Le Seuil, 1988

Badiou, A., *Manifeste pour la philosophie* (Manifesto for Philosophy), Paris, Le Seuil, 1989

Barlow, J.P., Cyberspace Declaration of Independence, Davos, Switzerland, 8 February 1996, **www.homes.eff.org/~barlow/Declaration-Final.html**

Baudrillard, J., *Simulacres et simulation*, Paris, Galilée, 1981

Baumeister, T., *De filosofie en de kunsten, Van Plato tot Beuys*, Nijmegen, Damon, 1999

Bayley, D.H. and Shearing, C.D., *The New Structure of Policing. Description, Conceptualization, and Research Agenda*, U.S. Department of Justice, 2001, **www.ncjrs.org/pdffiles1/nij/187083.pdf**

Becker, D., 'Army gunning for game players', 2004, **http://news.zdnet.com/2100-3513_22-5211682.html**

Benjamin, W., 'The Work of Art in the Age of Mechanical Reproduction' (1936), in: *Illuminations*, London, Pimlico, 1999

Berens, K. and Howard, G., *The Rough Guide to Videogaming*, London, Rough Guides Ltd., 2002

Berman, M., *All That Is Solid Melts into Air: The Experience of Modernity*, New York, Pinguin Books, 1988

Bey, H., *T.A.Z. The Temporary Autonomous Zone*, Ontological Anarchy, Poetic Terrorism, New York, Autonomedia, 1991

Bois, M., *Iannis Xenakis, The Man and His Music: A Conversation With the*

Composer and a Description of His Works, Westport, Greenwood Press, 1967

Bolter, J. and Grusin, R., *Remediation. Understanding New Media,* Cambridge/Massachusetts, The MIT Press, 1999

Boyer, M.C., *CyberCities: Visual Perception in the Age of Electronic Communication,* New York, Princeton Architectural Press, 1996

Boyer, M.C., Op de grens tussen steden en CyberCities, **www.dma.be/cvb/as/kino3/DFBOYER.htm**

Braembussche, van den A., *Denken over kunst. Een inleiding in de kunstfilosofie,* Bussum, uitgeverij Coutinho, 2000

Burroughs, W., *Naked Lunch* (1959), London, Flamingo, 1993

Burroughs, W., *Cities of the Red Night,* London, John Calder, 1981

Cassegård, C., 'After Paranoia', in: *Axess Magazine,* 2004, no. 9, **www.axess.se/english/archive/2004/nr9/currentissue/theme_cassegard.php**

Castells, M., *The Information Age: Economy, Society and Culture. The Rise of the Network Society,* Volume I, Oxford, Blackwell Publishers Ltd, 1996

Castells, M., *The Information Age: Economy, Society and Culture. The Power of Identity,* Volume II, Oxford, Blackwell Publishers Ltd, 1997

Castells, M., *The Information Age: Economy, Society and Culture. End of Millennium,* Volume III, Oxford, Blackwell Publishers Ltd, 1998

Castells, M. and Ince, M., *Conversations with Manuel Castells,* Cambridge, Polity Press, 2003

Cauter, de L., *The Capsular Civilization. On the City in the Age of Fear,* Rotterdam, NAi Publishers, 2004

Clover, C., 'Natural-born killers will not win hearts and minds', 2004, **www.christusrex.org/www1/news/ft-6-27-04.html**

Cobussen, M., 'De terreur van het oog', in: *De Groene Amsterdammer,* 10 January 1996

Cobussen, M., 'Verkenningen van/in een muzikale ruimte. Over Peter Sloterdijk en Edwin van der Heide', in: *Interakta #5, Grootstedelijke reflecties. Over kunst en openbare ruimte* (Oosterling, H.A.F and Thissen, S., eds.), Rotterdam, Faculteit der Wijsbegeerte van de Erasmus Universiteit, 2002

Cohen, S., *Visions of Social Control. Crime, Punishment and Classification,* Oxford, Polity Press, 1985

Cook, P., *Archigram,* London, Studio Vista Publishers, 1972

Cox, C. and Warner, D. (eds.), *Audio Culture. Readings in Modern Music,* New York, The Continuum International Publishing Group Inc, 2002

Cronly-Dillon, J. and Persaud, K.C., 'Blind subjects analyze visual images encoded in sound', in: *Journal of Physiology* 523P, no. 68, 2000

Curtis, W., *Le Corbusier: Ideas and Forms,* Oxford, Phaidon Press limited, 1986

Davis, E., Acoustic Cyberspace, 1997, **www.techgnosis.com/acoustic.html**

Davis, M., *City of Quartz. Excavating the Future In Los Angeles*, London, Pimlico, 1998

Davis, M., *Ecology of Fear. Los Angeles and the Imagination of Disaster*, New York, Vintage Books, 1999

Deamer, P., 'Branding the Architectural Author', in: *Perspecta* 37, 'Famous', Cambridge/London, MIT Press, 2005

Debord, G., *The Society of the Spectacle*, New York, Zone Books, 1994

Delanty, G., *Community*, London/New York, Routledge, 2003

Deleuze, G., *Différence et répétition* (Difference and Repetition), Paris, Presses Universitaires de France, 1968

Deleuze, G., *Pourparlers*. 1972–1990 (Negotiations. 1972–1990), Paris, Les éditions de Minuit, 1990

Deleuze, G. and Guattari, F., *Kafka. Pour une littérature mineure* (Kafka. Toward a Minor Literature), Paris, Les éditions de Minuit, 1975

Deleuze, G. and Guattari, F., *Mille plateaux. Capitalisme et schizophrénie* 2 (A Thousands Plateaux. Capitalism and Schizophrenia), Paris, Les éditions de Minuit, 1980

Deleuze, G. and Parnet, C., *Dialogues* (Dialogues), Paris, Flammarion, 1977

Dery, M., Black to the Future: Afro-futurism 1.0, **www.levity.com/markdery/black.html**

Diederichsen, D., 'Es streamt so sexy. Die Dialektiek von Clicks & Cuts', in: *Popvisionen. Links in die Zukunft* (Neumann-Braun, K., Schmidt A. and Mai, M., eds.), Frankfurt am Main, Suhrkamp, 2003

Diederichsen, D., Montage/Sampling/Morphing. On the Triad of Aesthetics/Technology/Politics, **www.medienkunstnetz.de/themes/image-sound_rela tions/montage_sampling_morphing/1**

During, E., 'Appropriations: Death of the Author In Electronic Music', in: *Sonic Process. A New Geography of Sounds* (Dàvila, M., ed.), Barcelona, Ingoprint, 2002

Edge Magazine, 'The Modern Age', The Mod Scene: What Happens When Gamers Build Games?, Bath, Future Publishing Ltd., 2003, no. 126

Eno, B., *A Year With Swollen Appendices: The Diary of Brian Eno*, London, Faber and Faber ltd, 1996

Eshun, K., *More Brilliant Than the Sun. Adventures in Sonic Fiction*, London, Quartet Books, 1998

Foucault, M., *Surveiller et Punir. Naissance de la prison* (Discipline and Punish. The Birth of the Prison), Paris, Gallimard, 1975

Foucault, M., *Histoire de la sexualité 1–La volonté de savoir* (The Will to

Knowledge), Paris, Gallimard, 1976

Foucault, M., *Histoire de la sexualité 2–L'usage des plaisirs* (The Use of Pleasure), Paris, Gallimard, 1984

Foucault, M., *Histoire de la sexualité 3–Le souci de soi* (The Care of the Self), Paris, Gallimard, 1984

Foucault, M., 'L'éthique du souci de soi comme practique de la liberté', in: *Dits et écrits*, Paris, Gallimard, 1994

Foucault, M., *Breekbare Vrijheid. Teksten & Interviews*, Amsterdam, Boom/Parrèsia, 2004

Galloway, A., *Protocol. How Control Exists after Decentralization*, Massachusetts, The MIT Press, 2004

Garland, D., *The Culture of Control. Crime and Social Order in Contemporary Society*, Oxford, Oxford University Press, 2001

Garner, J.S. (ed.), *The Company Town. Architecture and Society in the Early Industrial Age*, Oxford, Oxford University Press, 1992

Gibson, W., *Neuromancer*, London, HarperCollinsPublishers, 1993

Gibson, W., 'Modern boys and mobile girls', in: *The Observer*, 1 April 2001, **http://observer.guardian.co.uk/life/story/0,6903,466391,00.html**

Goldberg, B., *Oral History of Bertrand Goldberg, interviewed by Betty J. Blum*, Chicago, The Art Institute of Chicago, 1992, **www.artic.edu/aic/libraries/caohp/goldberg.pdf**

Graham, S. and Marvin, S., *Splintering Urbanism. Networked Infrastructures, Technological Mobilities and the Urban Condition*, London, Routledge, 2001

Grassmuck, V., 'I'm alone, but not lonely', 1990, **www.cjas.org/~leng/otaku-e.htm**

Gutierrez, L. and Portefaix, V., 'Homes for China', in: *Architectural Design* volume 75, 2005

Hall, S., 'What Is This "Black" in Black Popular Culture?', in: *Black Popular Culture* (Dent, G., ed.), Seattle, Bay Press, 1992

Hardt M., 'La société mondiale de contrôle', in: *Gilles Deleuze, une vie philosophique*, (Alliez, E., ed.), Le Plessis-Robinson, Synthélabo, 1998

Hardt, M. and Negri, T., *Empire*, Cambridge, Harvard University Press, 2000

Hardt, M. and Negri, T., *Multitude. War and Democracy in the Age of Empire*, New York, The Penguin Press, 2004

Hayward, K.J., *City Limits: Crime, Consumer Culture and the Urban Experience*, London, The Glass House, 2004

Hirsch, Von A. and Shearing, C., 'Exclusion from Public Space', in: *Ethical and Social Perspectives on Situational Crime Prevention*, Oxford, Hart Publishing, 2000

Jenkins, H., *Textual Poachers. Television Fans and Participatory Culture*, New York, Routledge, 1992

Johnson, S., *Everything Bad is Good for You*, London, Penguin Group, 2005

Jong, de A. and Schuilenburg, M.B., 'The world after Pong. On the dynamic of video games and their parallel cities', in: *Archis*, no. 3, Amsterdam, 2003

Jong, de A. and Schuilenburg, M.B., 'Scenius' contra Genius. Über das Umzingeln von Star-Architekten, in: *Bauwelt. Zeitschrift für Architekten*, no. 30, Berlin, 2004

Jong, de A. and Schuilenburg, M.B., 'De elektrificatie van de ruimte. Over de stedelijke kadans in elektronische muziek', in: *EasyCity. Interventies in een verscheurde stad* (Kallenberg, F., ed.), Amsterdam, De Vrije Ruimte, 2004

Jong, de A. and Schuilenburg, M.B., 'The audio-hallucinatory spheres of the city. A pop analysis of the urbanization process', in: *Open. Cahier on art and the public domain*, no. 9, Amsterdam, 2005

Jong, de A. and Schuilenburg, M.B., 'Virtuele oorlogsvoering. Oorlog en verzet in videogames', in: *Militaire Spectator*, no. 2, Breda, 2006   [169

Jong, de A. and Schuilenburg, M.B., 'From Genius to Scenius. Redefining creativity in the practice of architecture', in: *Game Set and Match II. On Computergames, Advanced Geometries, and Digital Technologies* (Oosterhuis, K. and Feireiss, L., eds.), Rotterdam, Episode Publishers, 2006

Jong, de A. and Schuilenburg, M.B., 'Pop-Up City', in: *Tank*, no. 7, London, 2006

Kent, S.L., *The Ultimate History of Video Games. From Pong to Pokémon and Beyond–The Story Behind the Craze That Touched Our Lives and Changed The World*, New York, Prima Publishing, 2001

King, L. (ed.), *Game On: The History and Culture of Videogame*, London, Laurence King Publishing Ltd, 2002

Kittler, F., *Gramophone, Film, Typewriter*, Stanford, Stanford University Press, 1999

Klein, N., *No Logo*, Flamingo, London, 2000

Klein, N., 'Reclaiming the Commons', in: *New Left Review* 9, May - June 2001, www.newleftreview.com/NLR24305.shtml

Koolhaas, R., *Delirious New York. A Retroactive Manifesto for Manhattan* (1978), Rotterdam, 010-Publishers, 1994

Kumar, A., 'America's Army game and the production of war', YCISS Working Paper number 27, 2004, www.yorku.ca/yciss/publications/documents/WP27-Kumar.pdf

Lenoir, T. and Lowood, H., 'Theaters of War: The Military-Entertainment

Complex', 2002, **www.stanford.edu/class/sts145/Library/Lenoir-Lowood_Thea tersOfWar.pdf**

Lesage, D., *Vertoog over verzet. Politiek in tijden van globalisering*, Antwerpen/Amsterdam, Meulenhoff/Manteau, 2004

Lessig, L., *Free Culture, How Big Media Uses Technology and the Law To Lock Down Culture and Control Creativity*, New York, The Penguin Press, 2004

Levander, M., 'Where Does Fantasy End?', in: *Time Magazine*, 2001, vol. 157, no. 22

Li, Z., 'The potential of America's Army the video game as civilian-military public sphere', 2003, **www.gamasutra.com/education/theses/20040725/ZLITH ESIS.pdf**

Lynch, K., *The Image of the City*, Cambridge/Massachusetts, The MIT Press, 1960

Manovich, L., *The Language of New Media*, Cambridge/Massachusetts, The MIT Press, 2002

McLuhan, M., *The Gutenberg Galaxy. The Making of Typographic Man*, London, Routledge & Kegan Paul, 1967

McLuhan, M. and Fiore, Q., *The Medium is the Message. An Inventory of Effects*, New York, Bantam Books, 1967

McLuhan, M. and Powers, B.R., *The Global Village. Transformations in World Life and Media in the 21st Century*, New York, Oxford University Press, 1989

Meyer, de G., 'De kritiek op videogames, met name inzake geweld', **www.ku leuven.ac.be/videogames/pop/pagina7.html**

Miller, P.D., *Rhythm Science*, Cambridge, The MIT Press, 2004

Mitchell, W.J., *City of Bits. Space, Place, and the Infobahn*, Cambridge/Massachusetts, The MIT Press, 1995

Mommaas, H. (i.c. Knulst, W. and Heuvel, van den M.), *De vrijetijdsindustrie in stad en land, een studie naar de markt van belevenissen*, WRR Voorstudies en achtergronden, Den Haag, SDU Uitgevers, 2000

Mosco, V., *The Digital Sublime. Myth, Power, and Cyberspace*, Cambridge/Massachusetts, The MIT Press, 2004

Mul, de J., *Cyberspace Odyssee*, Kampen, Uitgeverij Klement, 2002

Mulder, A., *Understanding Media Theory. Language, Image, Sound, Behaviour*, Rotterdam, V2_/NAi Publishers, 2004

Murakami, R., 'Japan's Lost Generation', in: *Time Magazine*, 1 May 2000, **www.time.com/time/asia/magazine/2000/0501/japan.essaymurakami.html**

Nelson, A., Introduction: Future Texts, in: *Social Text*, no. 71, Durham, Duke University Press, 2002

Neumann-Braun, K., Schmidt, A., Mai, M. (eds.), *Popvisionen. Links in die*

170]

Zukunft, Frankfurt am Main, Suhrkamp Verlag, 2003

Newman, J., *Videogames*, London, Routledge, 2004

News Tribune, 'Hezbollah computer game takes propaganda war on Israel to virtual battlefield', 2004, **www.newstribune.com/articles/2003/05/25/export 16774.txt**

Nieborg, D.B., 'Militaire Game(r)s: Vechten in de Virtuele Werkelijkheid', in: *Tijdschrift voor Mediageschiedenis*, Amsterdam, Boom, 2004

Ogg, A., *The Men Behind Def Jam. The Radical Rise of Russell Simmons and Rick Rubin*, London, Omnibus Press, 2002

Oosterling, H.A.F., *De opstand van het lichaam. Over verzet en zelfervaring bij Foucault en Bataille*, Amsterdam, SUA, 1989

Oosterling, H., 'Intermediality. Art between Images, Words, and Actions', in: *Think Art. Theory and Practice in the Arts of Today* (Marì, B. and Schaeffer, J.M., ed.), Rotterdam, Witte de With Center for Contemporary Art, 1998

Oosterling, H., *Radicale middelmatigheid*, Amsterdam, Boom, 2000

Pias, C., *Computer Spiel Welten*, München, Sequenzia Verlag, 2002

Provoost, M., Colenbrander, B., Alkemade, F., *Dutchtown. O.M.A.'s meesterproef in Almere*, Rotterdam, NAi Publishers, 1999

Rabinow, P. (ed.), *The Foucault Reader*, London, Penguin, 1984

Raessens, J., 'De virtuele ruimte. Computergames: interface van de eenentwintigste eeuw', in: *De ruimte*, bundel symposium 12 mei 2000, Studium Generale, Universiteit Utrecht, 2002

Raessens, J., 'Cinema and beyond. Film en het proces van digitalisering', in: *E-View*, no. 1, 2001

Reed, I., *Mumbo Jumbo* (1972), New York, Scribner, 1996

Reynolds, S., *Energy Flash. A Journey Through Rave Music and Dance Culture*, London, Picador, 1998

Rheingold, H., *The Virtual Community. Homesteading on the Electronic Frontier*, 1993, **www.rheingold.com/vc/book**

Riddell, R., 'Doom Goes To War', 1997, **www.wired.com/wired/archive/5.04/ff_doom_pr.html**

Rossi, A., *The Architecture of the City*, Cambridge/Massachusetts, The MIT Press, 1999

Russcol, H., *The Liberation of Sound: An Introduction to Electronic Music*, Englewood Cliffs, Prentice-Hall, 1972

Sassen, S., *The Global City: New York, London, Tokyo*, Princeton, Princeton University Press, 1991

Sassen, S., *Globalisering. Over mobiliteit van geld, mensen en informatie*, Amsterdam, Van Gennep, 1999

[171

Schafer, R.M., *The Soundscape. Our Sonic Environment and the Tuning of the World*, New York, Knopf, 1977

Shapiro, P. (ed.), *Modulations. A History of Electronic Music*, New York, Caipirinha Productions, 2000

Schuilenburg, M.B., 'In alle staten van beschuldiging. Straffen in een globale samenleving', in: *Nederlands Juristenblad*, no. 6, Den Haag, 2006

Schuilenburg, M.B., 'De kracht van een revolutie. Mensenrechten en de democratie', in: *Het Uur van de Waarheid. Alain Badiou—revolutionair denker* (Brabander, de R.A., ed.), Kampen, Ten Have, 2006

Schuilenburg, M.B., 'It's the protocol, stupid!', in: *Monu. Magazine on Urbanism*, no. 5, Kassel, 2006

Schuilenburg, M.B. and Jong, de A., 'De militarisering van de openbare ruimte. Over de invloed van videogames op onze werkelijkheid', in: *Justitiële verkenningen*, no. 4, Den Haag, 2005

Sloterdijk, P., *Im selben Boot. Versuch über die Hyperpolitik*, Frankfurt am Main, Suhrkamp, 1995

Sloterdijk, P., *Mediatijd*, (translation of: Der starke Grund, zusammen zu sein. Erinnerungen an die Erfindung des Volkes, Frankfurt am Main, Suhrkamp, 1998, and: Medien-Zeit. Drei Gegenwartsdiagnostische Versuche, Stuttgart, Cantz, 1993), Amsterdam, Boom, 1999

Sloterdijk, P., *Sphären I. Blasen, Mikrosphärologie*, Frankfurt am Main, Suhrkamp, 1998

Sloterdijk, P., *Regeln für den Menschenpark. Ein Antwortschreiben zu Heideggers Brief über den Humanismus*, Frankfurt am Main, Suhrkamp, 1999

Sloterdijk, P., *Sphären II. Globen, Makrosphärologie*, Frankfurt am Main, Suhrkamp, 1999

Sloterdijk, P., *Spären III. Schäume, Plurale Sphärologie*, Frankfurt am Main, Suhrkamp, 2004

Sloterdijk, P., *Im Weltinnenraum des Kapitals. Für eine philosophische Theorie der Globalisierung*, Frankfurt am Main, Suhrkamp, 2005

Sorkin, M., *Amazing Archigram*, New York, Metropolis Magazine, 1998

Tafuri, M., 'Machine et Mémoire: The City in the Work of Le Corbusier', in: *Le Corbusier: The Garland Essays* (Allen Brooks, H., ed.), New York, Garland Publishing, 1987

Thissen, S., 'Logboek van de bekladde stad. De stad als massamedium', in: *EasyCity. Interventies in een verscheurde stad*, (Kallenberg, F. ed.), Amsterdam, De Vrije Ruimte, 2004

Thissen, S., 'Wat is 'Urban Culture'? (My Adidas)', 2004/2005, **www.siebe thissen.net**

Toffler, A., *The Third Wave* (1980), New York, Bantam Books, 1990

Vidler, A., *Claude-Nicolas Ledoux. Architecture and Social Reform at the End of the Ancien Régime*, Cambridge/Massachusetts, The MIT Press, 1990

Virilio, P., *The Vision Machine*, Bloomington, Indiana University Press, 1995

Virno, P., *Public Sphere, Labour, Multitude. Strategies of Resistance in Empire*, Seminar organised by Officine Precarie in Pisa, 2003, **www.generation-online.org/t/common.htm**

Wakin, D.J., 'Video Game Mounts Simulated Attacks Against Israeli Targets', 2003, **www.nytimes.com/2003/05/18/international/middleeast/18VIDE.html?ex=1368590400&en=d04c67f3901c3721&ei=5007&partner=USERLAND**

Weeber, C., *Het wilde wonen*, Rotterdam, 010-Publishers, 1998

Wogenscky, A., 'The Unité d'Habitation at Marseille', in: *Le Corbusier: The Garland Essays* (Allen Brooks, H., ed.), New York, Garland Publishing, 1987

Žižek, S., *Looking Awry. An Introduction to Jacques Lacan Through Popular Culture*, Cambridge/Massachusetts, The MIT Press, 1991

Žižek, S., *Het subject en zijn onbehagen. Vijf essays over psychoanalyse en het cartesiaanse cogito*, Amsterdam, Boom, 1997

Žižek, S., *Welcome to the Desert of the Real: Five Essays on September 11 and Related Dates*, London/New York, Verso, 2002

[173

Index

KUMA WAR ★

AL WAR NEWS. REAL WAR GAMES

Ramadi جسر عتاق

Screenshot of 'Battlezone', p. 24

The 'EST 2000' training system. The training can be carried out with various weapons, such as pistols, (machine) guns, anti-tank artillery, and bazookas.

TROOPS

MOUT 101

FRONT

LINKS

GAME

PRESS

WEAPONS

WARRIOR

07:21.14

PLAYBOOK:

Learn urban combat techniques.

189

NEW TRAILER:

Watch the latest Full Spectrum Warrior trailer.

COMMERCIALS:

All the latest FSW commercials are now online.

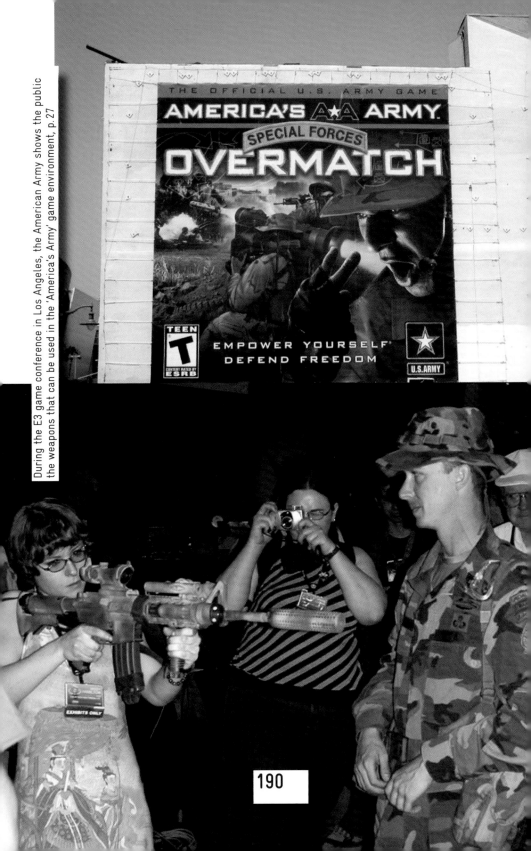

During the E3 game conference in Los Angeles, the American Army shows the public the weapons that can be used in the 'America's Army' game environment, p. 27

FULL SPECTRUM WARRIOR

Cover of 'Full Spectrum Warrior', p. 27–29

6+
pegi.info

PANDEMIC

THQ

MILITARY CHECKPOINT
PREPARE TO STOP

The 'Mission Rehearsal Exercise' simulation (2001) in which aspiring soldiers go on a mission to a city in Bosnia. A curved screen measuring 3 metres by 10 is drawn up around the players.

194

Map of 'Special Forces Dockside Eastern Approach' from 'America's Army', p. 36–37

● Random Spawn Points   ● Random Objectives

SF Dockside Eastern Approach

Enemy forces have shipped a set of containers holding biological agents in (UWAO) Brandy, vicinity grid HW092176. Friendly motorized forces ordered to secure and evacuate the components have been delayed from reaching the site due to a major storm just of the coast that is expected to make landfall within the hour. It is feared that enemy forces will return and attempt to retrive the components before they can be intercepted.

Map of 'Urban Assault West' from 'America's Army', p. 36–37

Assault West Deploy

West Objective

Assault East Deploy

Urban Assault West

A coalition convoy was raided and the cargo was stolen. It has been confirmed that the insurgents and the cargo are based in a residential area of the city. Due to the dense urban nature of the area it will be necessary to do a house by house assault on foot. A squad from the 172nd Sep. Infantry BDE must conduct an assault to take and hold objectives cargo ALPHA and BRAVO. Once objectives are captured wait for arrival of friendly reinforcements to transport cargo.

AMERICA'S ARMY

Global Information Grid

An integrated, interoperable worldwide network of information technology products and management services that processes and moves information.

195

OUTSIDE THE GATE (DII)	INSIDE THE GATE (BII)	LAST 400 FEET	INFO APPLIANCES

Workstations
PCs,
Peripherals,
Fax's
VTC Suites
Phones
PWCS

"To-the-Wall"

Integrity - Service - Excellence

16

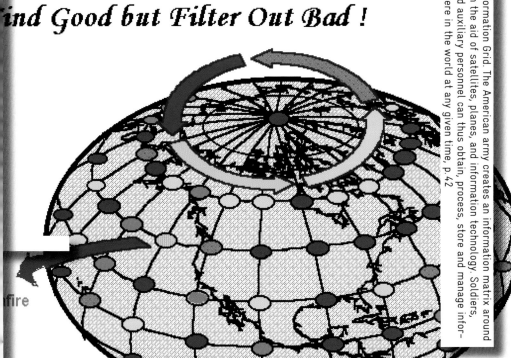

Find Good but Filter Out Bad !

fire

The Global Information Grid. The American army creates an information matrix around the Earth with the aid of satellites, planes, and information technology. Soldiers, politicians and auxiliary personnel can thus obtain, process, store and manage information anywhere in the world at any given time, p. 42

SECURITY CAMERA #375

Surveillance camera, p. 40–43, 55, 57

The Steadicopter is an unmanned helicopter that was developed by the Israeli company 'Steadicopter'. The helicopter offers various possibilities: monitoring, traffic control, photography in areas difficult to reach, and immigration control.

EP-3E spy plane

Guardian CL-327 surveillance robot

Gun and pistol shot detector

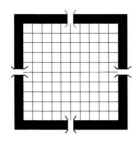

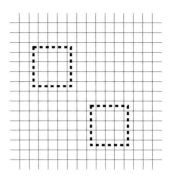

PANOPTICON   URBAN CONTAINER   E-CITY

Aurora 3D, software by means of which cameras can recognize faces, p. 40–43, 55, 57

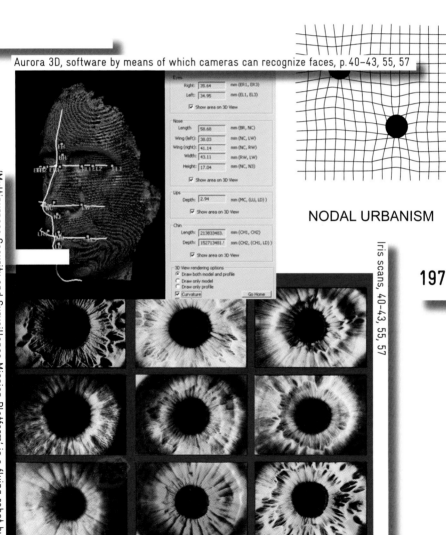

NODAL URBANISM

'Multipurpose Security and Surveillance Mission Platform' is a flying robot by means of which targets can be destroyed without endangering the life of a human pilot.

Iris scans, 40–43, 55, 57

WALLED CITY

COMPANY TOWN

Palmanova,
Savorgano, Lorini &
Scamozzi,
Italy (1593)

Pullman Town,
Chicago (1880)

Offices
Restaurants
Hotel
Sauna
Universit
Theatre Haird
chool P
Swimmin
aycare cen
Church P
Concertha
Record
Golf

Freedom Ship,
Norman Nixon,
(2010)

Congestion Charge Zone,
London (2003)

E-CITY

City Walk,
The Jerde Partnership,
Los Angeles, USA (1993)

Dutch pavilion EXPO2000,
MVRDV,
Hannover, Germany (2000)

West Edmor.
Alberta, Car

THEMED CITY

Chicago Temple Building,
Holabird & Roche,
Chicago (1924)

...m Building,
...Sullivan,
...(1890)

Rockefeller Center,
Corbett, Harrison & Hood,
New York (1932)

New York Hospital,
Coolidge, Shepley,
Richardson & Abbott,
New York (1932)

Dhahran,
Saudi Arabia (1935)

COMPOUND

Unité d'Habitation,
Le Corbusier,
Marseille (1952)

Marina City,
Bertrand Goldberg,
Chicago (1964)

CITY WITHIN A CITY

Housebuilding project in Happy Valley, Hong Kong, China, p. 53-55

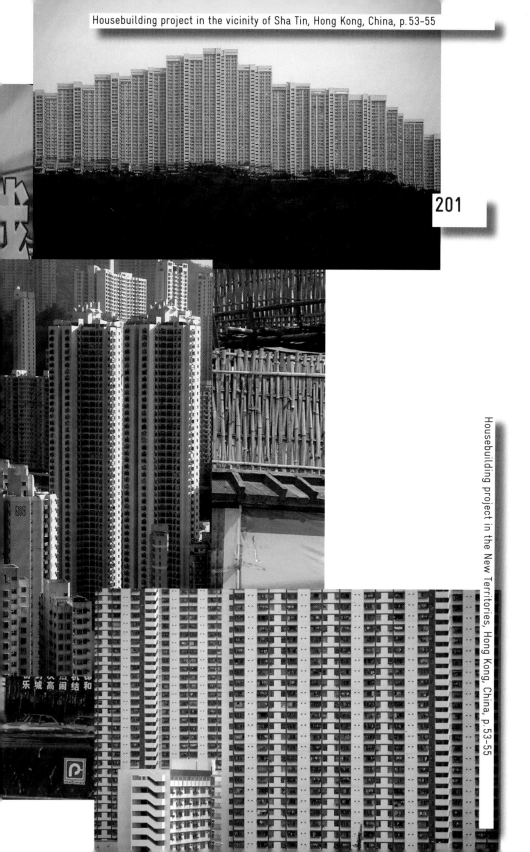

Housebuilding project in the New Territories, Hong Kong, China, p. 53-55

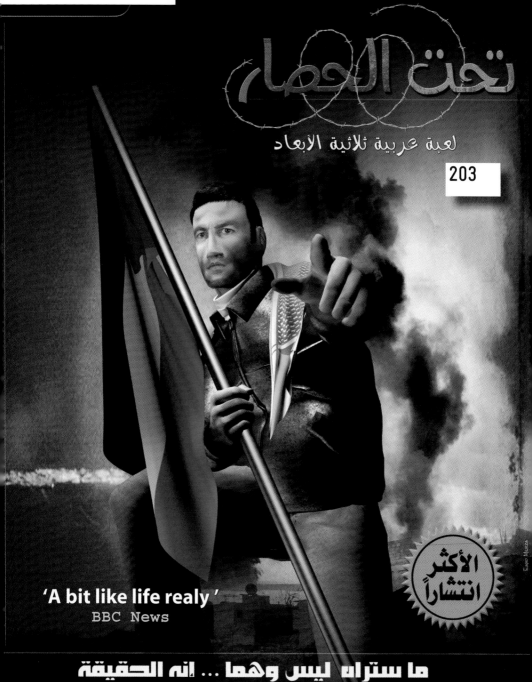

تحت الحصار

لعبة عربية ثلاثية الأبعاد

الأكثر
انتشاراً

'A bit like life realy'
BBC News

ما ستراه ليس وهما ... إنه الحقيقة

ملحمة إنسانية نضعها أمانة بين يديك كي لا تنسى... أرضك وجذورك

تحت الحصار وتحت الرماد اسماء تجاريان مملوكان لأفكار ميديا ويخظيان بحماية قوانين تنظيم الملكية الفكرية في العالم

تم تطوير هذا المنتج في مختبرات شركة أفكار ميديا - توزيع دار الفكر - دمشق

تأليف و إخراج رضوان قاسمية

PC
CD
ROM

13+

Screenshots of 'Velvet-Strike', p. 66, 157 n. 43

rainbow bright   C0un7D0wn
rainbow bright   [MO@M]Dirty Harry
=^^I Love You@Q@^^=   rainbow bright

=^^I Love You@Q@^^= attacked a teammate
Noob (RADIO): Fire in the hole!
[MO@M]Dirty Harry attacked a teammate
=^^I Love You@Q@^^= attacked a teammate

205

Advert for hubcaps, p. 85–86

MOBB DEEP

TEL: 323.889.4350 FAX: 323
www.makaveliwhee

RAZOR   BLINK   VIPER

G3   GAME   RODEO 5

TRIUNFO 7   TRIUNFO 5   ZAINT

BLAZE   TWISTER   GTO

S. 5" INCH LIP AVAILABLE IN SOME APPLICATIONS. DEALER INQUIRIES W

Advert for the South Pole brand of clothes, with the members of the hip-hop group Mobb Deep as models. The advert announced their album 'Amerikaz Nightmare' at the same time.

ALBUM IN STORES NOW!

207

A REVOLUTION IN QUALITY DIAMO

Watches of the Joe Rodeo brand, inlaid with diamonds, p. 85-86

SOUTH POLE®

AUTHENTIC CLOTHING COLLECTION
FOR MORE INFORMATION CALL: 1-800-357-4989

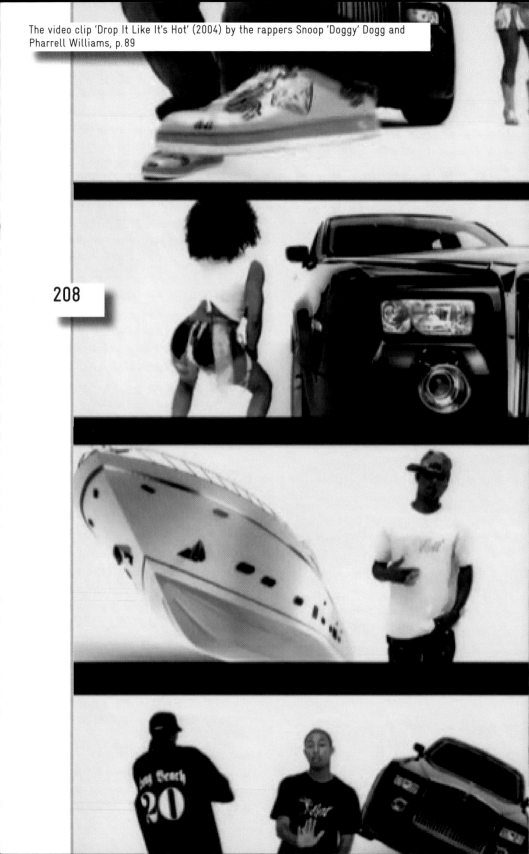

Postcard architecture (Guggenheim, Prada shop, Seattle Public Library, Phaeno Science Museum, Swiss Re Tower), p. 75

213

Flash architect George Lucas (Sci-Fi), p. 117

Locations Map
*Relative distances not to scale

Dantooine
Yavin IV
Ord Mantell
Ithor
Ryloth
Yavin
Outer Rim
Mid Rim
Mon Calamari
Wild Space
Inner Rim
Core Worlds
Kuat
Kashyyyk
Rodia
Coruscant
Deep Core
Alderaan
Colonies
Chandrila
Hutt Space
Kessel
Corellia
Exploration Region
Arisnar
Sullust
Nal Hutta
Nar Shaddaa

215

95

Viruses, p. 104

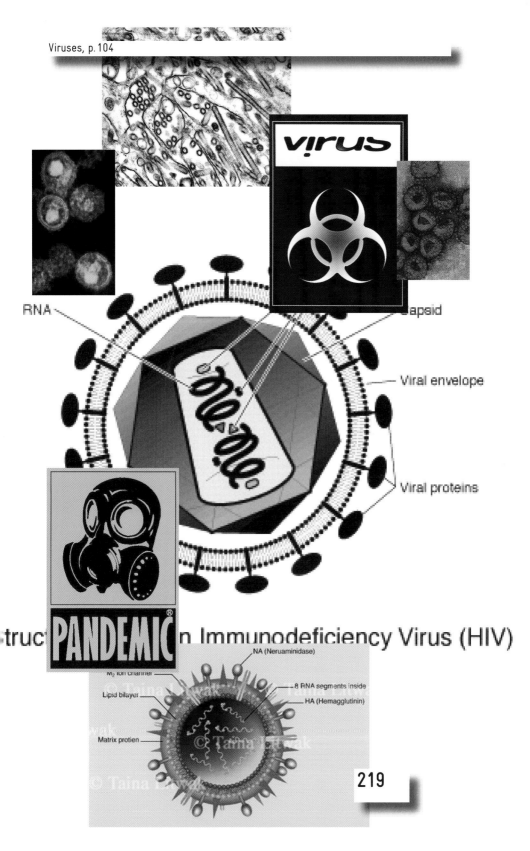

RNA

Capsid

Viral envelope

Viral proteins

Structure of Human Immunodeficiency Virus (HIV)

NA (Neruaminidase)

M₂ ion channel

Lipid bilayer

8 RNA segments inside

HA (Hemagglutinin)

Matrix protien

219

Central network, p. 125

Decentral network, p. 125

Distributed network, p. 125

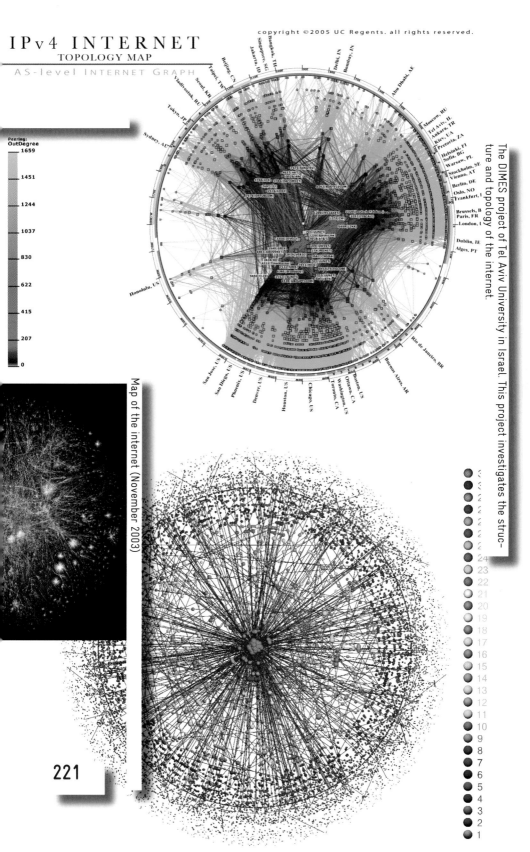

IPv4 INTERNET
TOPOLOGY MAP
AS-level INTERNET GRAPH

The DIMES project of Tel Aviv University in Israel. This project investigates the structure and topology of the internet.

Peering: OutDegree

1659
1451
1244
1037
830
622
415
207
0

Map of the internet (November 2003)

221

Open Source, p. 120–124

BlobFlow
Vorticity for all

FREE CULTURE

Open Project

Project Management Software
For Linux

BY:

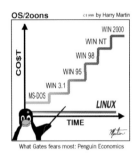

OS/2oons   ©1998 by Harry Martin

What Gates fears most: Penguin Economics

https://dsl.org/copyleft/dsl.txt

info♦narchy

222

THE DOOM WIKI

open source ™

IDEAS

mapster

Open Source

WoWWiki

WIKIPEDIA
The Free Encyclopedia

The evolution of 'Counterstrike', p. 118–120

ACTION QUAKE2

Tom Clancy's **RAINBOW SIX**

HALF-LIFE

STEAM™

WON

Enemy [cHc](!@#$^&%)

HALF-LIFE²

COUNTER STRIKE

'Counterstrike': choice of weapons

'Counterstrike': choice of teams

Environment of 'Fy_poolday' in 'Counterstrike' (designed by ivan300)

226

name Gordon, Gary's Mod, The Trenches, Red Orchestra, Natural Selection, Brainbread Minerva, Ragdoll Kungfu, Earth Special Forces, Dystopia), p. 118–120

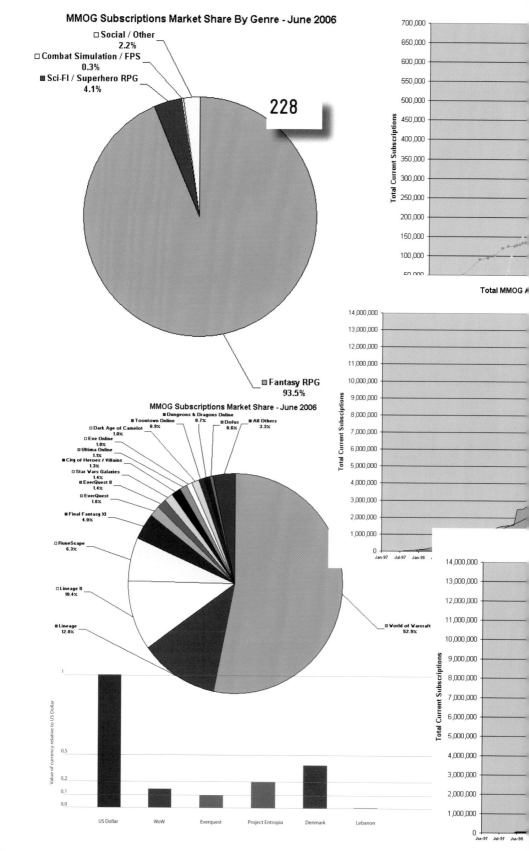

MMOG Subscriptions Market Share By Genre - June 2006

- □ Social / Other 2.2%
- □ Combat Simulation / FPS 0.3%
- ■ Sci-FI / Superhero RPG 4.1%

228

■ Fantasy RPG 93.5%

MMOG Subscriptions Market Share - June 2006

- ■ Dungeons & Dragons Online 0.7%
- ■ Toontown Online 0.9%
- □ Dofus 0.6%
- ■ All Others 3.3%
- □ Dark Age of Camelot 1.0%
- □ Eve Online 1.0%
- □ Ultima Online 1.1%
- ■ City of Heroes / Villains 1.3%
- □ Star Wars Galaxies 1.4%
- ■ EverQuest II 1.4%
- □ EverQuest 1.6%
- ■ Final Fantasy XI 4.0%
- □ RuneScape 6.3%
- □ Lineage II 10.4%
- ■ Lineage 12.0%
- □ World of Warcraft 52.9%

Total Current Subscriptions

Total MMOG /

Jan-97 Jul-97 Jan-98

Value of currency relative to US Dollar

US Dollar   WoW   Everquest   Project Entropia   Denmark   Lebanon

Jan-97 Jul-97 Jan-98

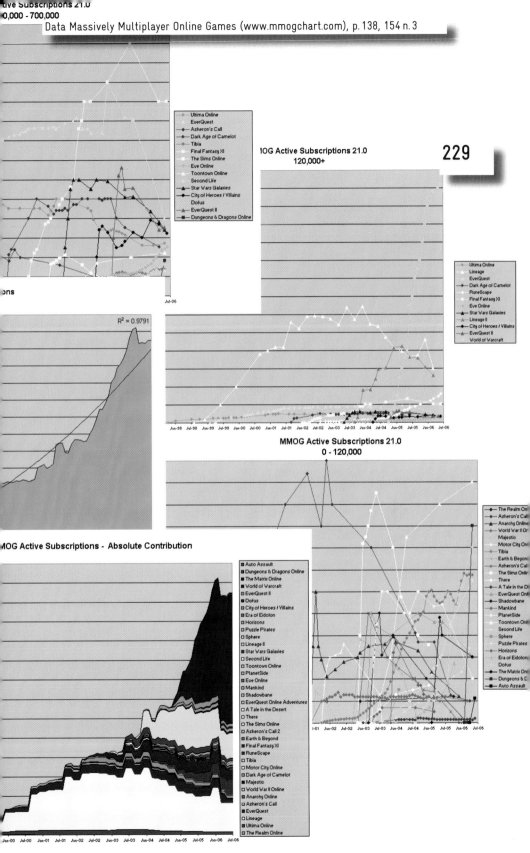

The virtual economy of Massively Multiplayer Online Roleplaying Games, p. 138

Exchange Rate of WOW Gold to USD (Weekly Average, Mar)

WOW US

Exchange Rate of WOW Gold to USD (Weekly Average, Mar)

WOW EU

Exchange Rate of Ultima Gold to USD (Weekly Average, Mar)

Ultima Online

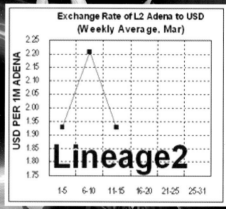

Exchange Rate of L2 Adena to USD (Weekly Average, Mar)

Lineage2

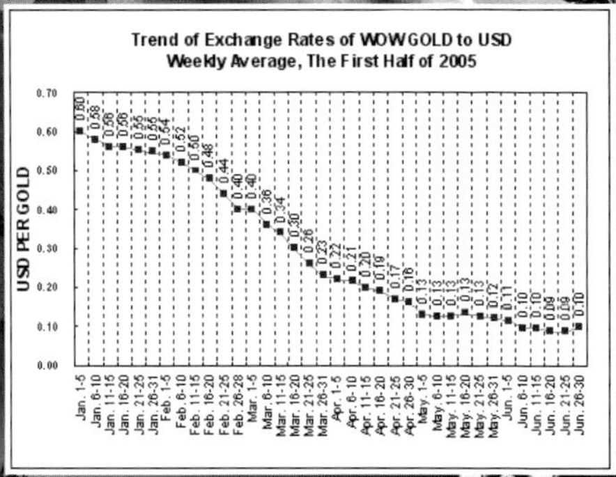
Trend of Exchange Rates of WOWGOLD to USD
Weekly Average, The First Half of 2005
USD PER GOLD

30 Day Gold
February 15, 2006 to March 17, 2006
HIGH $568.60 on Mar 03,2006 LOW $535.00 on Mar 10, 2006
NY Close
London AM
London PM
$U.S. per ounce
www.kitco.com

SPECIALIZE
YOUR

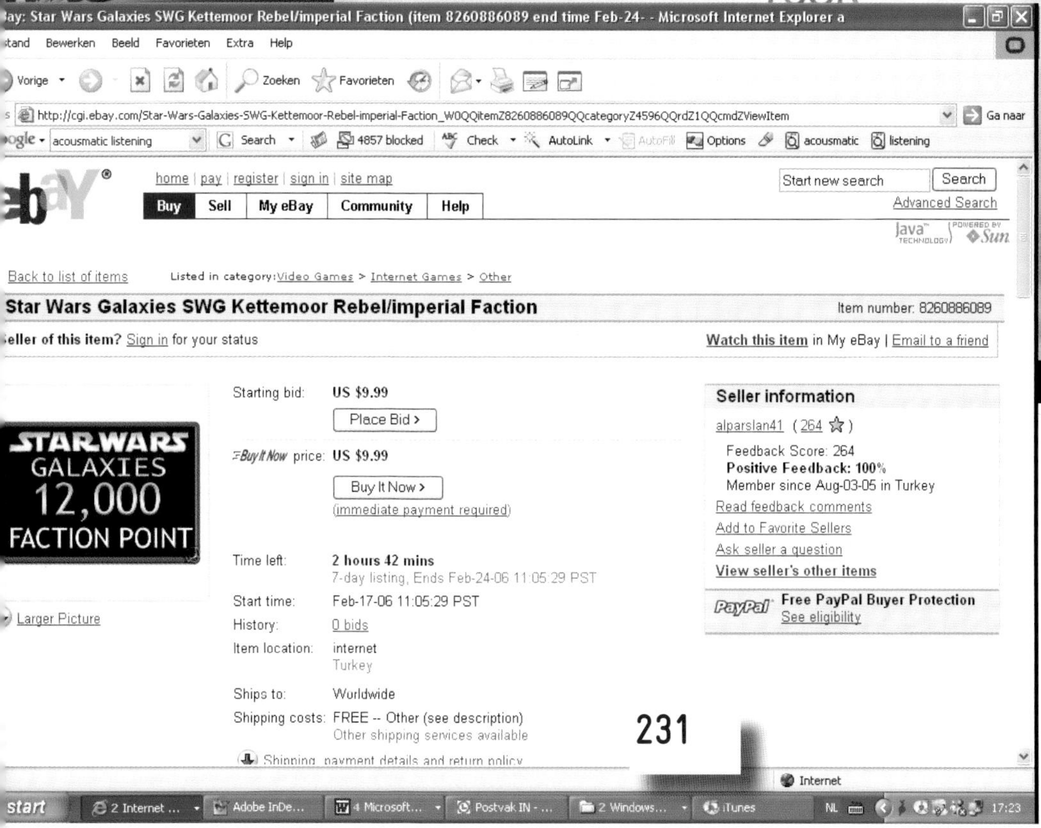
ay: Star Wars Galaxies SWG Kettemoor Rebel/imperial Faction (item 8260886089 end time Feb-24- - Microsoft Internet Explorer a
http://cgi.ebay.com/Star-Wars-Galaxies-SWG-Kettemoor-Rebel-imperial-Faction_W0QQitemZ8260886089QQcategoryZ4596QQrdZ1QQcmdZViewItem
home | pay | register | sign in | site map
Buy Sell My eBay Community Help
Start new search Search
Advanced Search
Back to list of items Listed in category: Video Games > Internet Games > Other
Star Wars Galaxies SWG Kettemoor Rebel/imperial Faction
Item number: 8260886089
eller of this item? Sign in for your status
Watch this item in My eBay | Email to a friend
STAR WARS GALAXIES 12,000 FACTION POINT
Larger Picture
Starting bid: US $9.99
Place Bid >
Buy It Now price: US $9.99
Buy It Now >
(immediate payment required)
Time left: 2 hours 42 mins
7-day listing, Ends Feb-24-06 11:05:29 PST
Start time: Feb-17-06 11:05:29 PST
History: 0 bids
Item location: internet
Turkey
Ships to: Worldwide
Shipping costs: FREE -- Other (see description)
Other shipping services available
Seller information
alparslan41 (264)
Feedback Score: 264
Positive Feedback: 100%
Member since Aug-03-05 in Turkey
Read feedback comments
Add to Favorite Sellers
Ask seller a question
View seller's other items
Free PayPal Buyer Protection
See eligibility

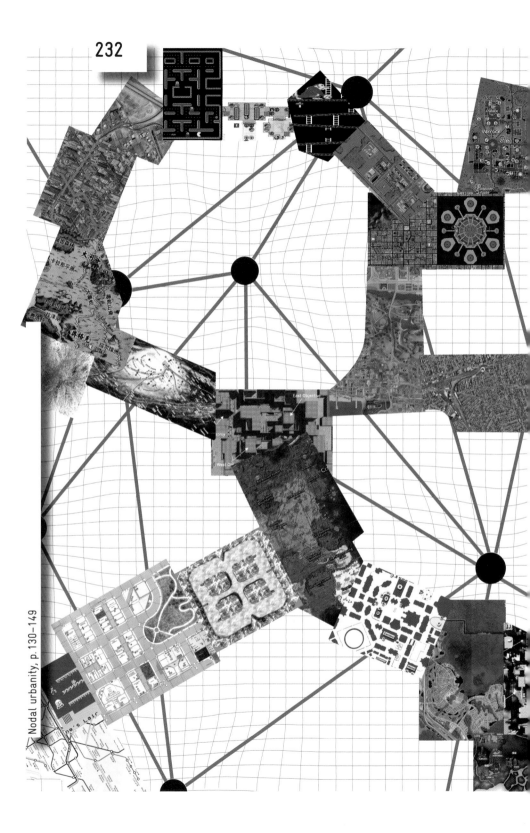